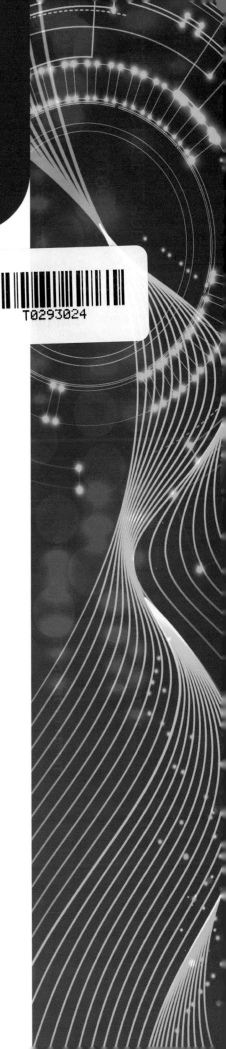

FUTURESCAN

Health Care Trends and Implications

2025

T0293024

Leveraging Technology and Innovation to Advance Value-Based Care

Ian Morrison, PhD

As artificial intelligence (AI) continues to reshape society as we know it, health care leaders are presented with an ever-increasing array of possibilities for transforming the delivery and reimbursement of services. The ideas and strategies presented in this edition of *Futurescan* may cover a broad range of topics, but they all lead to a common set of goals: reducing health care costs, improving health outcomes, and enhancing the patient experience.

The eight subject matter experts in this publication explore value-based care financing models, new imperatives in strategic planning, community collaborations for improving social determinants of health, changing workforce expectations, sustainability for smaller hospitals, and advances in digital behavioral health and predictive technologies. Their insights will promote meaningful discussions among health care leaders who guide hospitals and health systems in meeting the needs of local stakeholders and of staff members on the front lines of delivering care.

While perusing these informative articles, readers will have the opportunity to take the pulse of their colleagues nationwide regarding these topics via the results of the annual *Futurescan*

survey, which is administered as part of this publication. As health care becomes more complex, the wisdom of these thought leaders and the collective opinions of hospital and health system executives around the country should assist organizations in planning for the next five years.

Behavioral Health's Digital Future

While the percentage of total health care expenditures devoted to behavioral health remains in the single digits,

mental health conditions continue to affect the total cost of care in the United States. Behavioral health expenditures total $188 billion while driving four times the medical spend for patients suffering from co-occurring behavioral and chronic health conditions. Mike Rhoades, chief executive officer (CEO) of Alera Health, notes that while many hospitals and health systems experience this financial drain, organizations without behavioral health services are impacted the most by patients with mental health conditions.

About the Subject Matter Expert

Ian Morrison, PhD, is an author, consultant, and futurist. He received an undergraduate degree from the University of Edinburgh, Scotland; a graduate degree from the University of Newcastle upon Tyne, England; and an interdisciplinary doctorate in urban studies from the University of British Columbia, Canada. He is the author of several books, including the best-selling *The Second Curve: Managing the Velocity of Change.* Morrison is the former president of the Institute for the Future and a founding partner of Strategic Health Perspectives, a forecasting service for clients in the health care industry.

Notably, the highest utilization of telehealth is for accessing behavioral health services, with 37 percent of patients using it to connect to providers. However, digital health can also involve mobile apps, remote monitoring, avatars, and wearables. Patients with more severe mental health disorders are frequently the most difficult to engage in treatment. Hospitals and health systems that are committed to value-based care arrangements are finding that these technologies reduce the overall cost of care and improve patient outcomes. Digital health tools have been especially useful in operationalizing partnerships with specialty providers of behavioral health in areas where no therapists are physically located. Once the services are in place, these partnerships can result in downstream cost efficiencies by using digital tools to facilitate communication, care coordination, data sharing, and analytics so that patients have to tell their story only once to their primary care provider as they move through the system of care. Any organization can also benefit by strengthening the provider–patient connection through the use of these tools.

The Use of Predictive Technologies

AI is rapidly transforming many facets of our daily existence, including commerce, social connections, and law enforcement. Health care is no exception, with a recent finding that AI—also known as predictive technologies—has the potential to deliver an astounding $1 trillion of improvements in the health care setting. The many applications of AI have made Roberta L. Schwartz, PhD, MHS, FACHE, chief innovation officer of the Houston Methodist hospital system, an enthusiastic proponent who is exploring how it can create the hospital of the future.

Schwartz believes that predictive technologies can support clinicians in streamlining care delivery, reducing their workload, and multiplying their surrogates to alleviate shortages of nurses, advanced practice providers, and physicians. Fixed digital cameras in rooms are allowing for centralized monitoring

programs to supply a new level of patient oversight and facilitate staff communications. Rural hospitals especially will benefit from this technology. Remote patient monitoring is already saving the lives of patients—both inside and outside the hospital setting.

The ability to create personalized risk profiles based on huge numbers of Medicare patient records allows clinicians to identify which patients may need additional care and follow-up. Remote monitoring is moving beyond a fragmented, disease-specific use to a single common platform that broadens the range of data that can be viewed and analyzed remotely.

As with any level of change, staff resistance can pose problems, but Schwartz says that reminding all stakeholders of the benefits of the specific innovation can be powerful and persuasive.

Community Benefit

According to Len M. Nichols, PhD, nonresident fellow at the Urban Institute and professor emeritus of health policy at George Mason University, community benefit activities should advance the health and well-being of every individual in the country. A national discussion on how health care community-benefit dollars should be spent is occurring in tandem with the emergence of new models of how community partners can best collaborate to

improve individuals' ability to achieve better health. These partnerships often focus on social determinants of health such as housing, food insecurity, and other social and economic needs. Their efforts build on hospitals' and health systems' long-standing commitment to serving the health needs of their communities.

Nichols says that engaging with local residents to learn what their health priorities are has been one of the biggest community benefit trends over the last 20 years. By taking the data and insights gained from the community health needs assessment process, hospitals and health systems are making strong commitments to address and improve social determinants of health. These initiatives often include input from community members on the design of interventions and their evaluation, leading to better relationships and outcomes. Through this process, hospitals and health systems are becoming powerful catalysts for change that uplift entire populations and invest in the health and well-being of all members of a community.

Disruption in the Era of Value Based Care

Value-based care, also known as accountable care, became the preferred payment model when the Centers for Medicare and Medicaid Services (CMS) established the CMS Innovation Center in 2010 to identify ways to improve health care quality and reduce costs. Although some health care organizations have shifted their operations to work within a reimbursement model that pays for value rather than volume, the adoption of accountable care nationwide has been relatively slow. CMS and commercial payers continue to reimburse under the more lucrative fee-for-service arrangement that rewards the provision of more—not fewer—services.

MemorialCare began developing the infrastructure that supports accountable care in 2014. Barry Arbuckle, president and CEO, characterizes value-based care as performing procedures at the right site of care (both clinically and financially) for the patient, even when the reimbursement is lower. When a health system takes on full risk for the care of a defined population, it is essential to increase the number and kinds of access points along the continuum of care. MemorialCare has built an extensive portfolio of digital and virtual care assets that can link patients to the appropriate level of medical and behavioral health care services.

In 2017 the organization signed its first full-risk direct-to employer contract, which requires patients to select a MemorialCare provider. Early engagement with these patients is facilitated by a handheld device that enables remote physical exams from the home, leading to earlier diagnosis of any underlying health issues. The partnership has resulted in dramatic decreases in admissions, pharmacy costs, and total cost of care. MemorialCare has used the results from this first contractual relationship to attract 10 additional direct-to-employer contracts.

Arbuckle advises that health care leaders educate their boards of directors and leadership teams on what it means to be paid for outcomes and value rather than for volume. A different infrastructure is required. An essential component of successfully implementing a value-based model is data collection and analytics, which provides an accurate assessment of the organization's medical cost ratio. Equally important is an understanding of the criticality

of patient engagement and access. In contractual relationships, insurance plan design matters because it drives consumer behavior.

Healthcare Employees' Changing Expectations

Recruitment and retention continue to be among the foremost issues of concern for health care leaders nationwide. America now has four very different generations within its workforce, all with unique expectations for their employment. Hanna Patterson—senior vice president of healthcare and applied learning at Guild, a company that partners with employers to offer education and upskilling—provides an overview of the emerging requirements of health care workers and how hospitals and health systems can retain and attract current and prospective employees. She says that most hospital leaders would be surprised to learn that the vast majority of workers would prefer to stay with their current employer if their needs were being met.

Many younger workers are looking for more flexibility to accommodate family demands or school schedules. Staff members also want their employers to take an actionable interest in their growth and development. To meet this need, some hospitals have introduced talent development channels that focus on educating entry-level workers to successfully graduate into higher level positions through tuition-free programs, clinical career pathways, and personalized coaching. Overall personnel shortages have motivated some health care organizations to reconsider

populations they might have previously discounted—such as those without high school diplomas—who can be mentored and trained along a predefined pipeline of development.

Patterson is also seeing an organizational commitment to equity and inclusion in the workplace. She cites the example of one health system that created a program to develop a more equitable and representative nursing population to meet the needs of its multiethnic community. These initiatives have significant community benefit implications for entire populations because education, income, and job opportunities positively affect health access and quality of life. Some hospitals are including these initiatives in their community benefits reporting.

Overall, Patterson says it is critical for an organization to have a vision of where its workforce is headed and to consider the types of positions and care team models it will need in the future.

All-Payer Reimbursement Rate-Setting Models

Tori Bayless, CEO of Luminis Health in Annapolis, discusses the state of Maryland's various initiatives for managing the total cost of care (TCOC) for defined populations. These initiatives began with the 1971 mandate granting Maryland's Health Services Cost Review Commission the authority to set hospital- and service-specific rates statewide. Her insights are invaluable for any health system executives who are considering accepting fixed, lump-sum payments to cover the costs of all

inpatient and outpatient care delivered to a predefined population of patients. These lessons are especially relevant for organizations that are considering participation in CMS's new payment initiative, the States Advancing All-Payer Health Equity Approaches and Development (AHEAD) model. AHEAD focuses on lowering overall health care expenditures, reducing health inequities, and improving patient outcomes. It would provide participating hospitals with a set rate to provide medical services to a predetermined population of Medicaid enrollees, certain Medicare beneficiaries, and people who are covered by one or more private payers.

Bayless has several suggestions for organizations that are considering the AHEAD model. Health care leaders should know that the model's focus is on primary care, health equity, care transformation, and TCOC for Medicare enrollees. These enrollees may have no control over the costs incurred outside their system yet may still be responsible for them. Growing volume and market share are not aligned with AHEAD, which prioritizes keeping patients out of the hospital. Hospital leaders should be prepared to accept a level of shared accountability and decision-making with a coalition consisting of payers, providers, representatives from the state department of health, and elected officials. Evaluation of these programs and processes will be ongoing.

Strategic Planning

Jim Cotelingam, chief strategy officer at Cleveland Clinic, provides salient advice for health care leaders who are creating or updating their organizations' five-year strategic plans. While these essential documents set the roadmap for growth and economic sustainability, the ever-changing health care environment requires that new realities be factored into strategic planning. Cotelingam believes that AI is a game changer with the potential to revolutionize both clinical and administrative operations.

These include electronic health record documentation, the diagnosis of medical conditions, and many other use cases. Cybersecurity and the protection of digital information have also risen to the top of Cotelingam's priority list. Workforce planning is complicated by the emergence of private equity bidding for specialists and of payers such as United and Optum, who are pursuing vertical integration.

Cotelingam cautions that growth does not necessarily deliver the same results that it did in the past. Existing service lines and markets also require resources, and if they are reliable sources of revenue, it may be prudent to nurture them instead of new service lines. A strategic plan must also anticipate the effects of new financial and reimbursement models and payment reform, particularly in light of potential changes resulting from upcoming elections. Finally, it is essential to employ an approach that integrates strategic, financial, and capital planning based on data analysis. This will help create shared organizational visions and commitments rather than an isolated strategic plan.

The Survival of Small Organizations

Of the 1,649 community-based hospitals in the United States, 32 percent are unaffiliated with a health system, presenting unique challenges for sustainability. Dave Schreiner, president and CEO of Katherine Shaw Bethea, says that several key performance indicators can predict whether an organization can capitalize appropriately or not, with the most accurate being an organization's day's cash metric. Ongoing underperformance in this area could be the bellwether for considering a partnership or affiliation.

Variable costs provide the only opportunity to align expense structures with projected reimbursement. Schreiner believes that health care leaders in small organizations may need to make hard choices, such as scaling back or

eliminating services if cash flow becomes a challenge. But before doing so, organizations must factor in the downstream cost of closing a service. The potential penalties for readmissions could exceed savings.

Other options include outsourcing to reduce personnel expenses and finding new lines of business. Schreiner has successfully recruited specialists to come to his campus and provide services that were previously unavailable in the community, which benefits patients as well as the provider, which may not have previously had access to those patients.

When an affiliation becomes a viable possibility, Schreiner says it is important to manage the expectations of both the board of directors and the community. The leaders of independent hospitals often live among the people they serve, and they know what their community needs. It is incumbent on them to provide it, whether as an independent organization or in an affiliation with a health system.

Conclusion

As CMS moves our nation ever closer to a reimbursement model focused on value-based care, C-suite executives have many considerations as they prepare for a payment system that rewards value and not volume. The accountable care experiences of the subject matter experts featured in this issue of *Futurescan* should prove instructive during these deliberations. The technological advances they highlight will also be essential considerations for future strategic planning. To add to the complexity, election results at the local, state, and federal levels have the potential to alter or add government mandates on reproductive services, care access, and health care funding.

In the current health care environment, hospital and health system leaders will find *Futurescan 2025* to be an invaluable resource that is grounded in the experience of thought leaders and in the opinions of their colleagues nationwide.

Building Your Five-Year Growth Plan

with Jim Cotelingam, Chief Strategy Officer, Cleveland Clinic

Strategic planning in health care has traditionally involved a comprehensive analysis of an organization's strengths, weaknesses, opportunities, and threats, which is then used to identify areas of improvement and develop strategies to help the organization achieve its goals over the next several years. A good strategic plan helps the organization adapt to the ever-changing health care environment, align its resources with its goals, set priorities, and make difficult decisions. But given the current economic picture and trends in the health care industry, what is the value of a traditional five-year strategic plan?

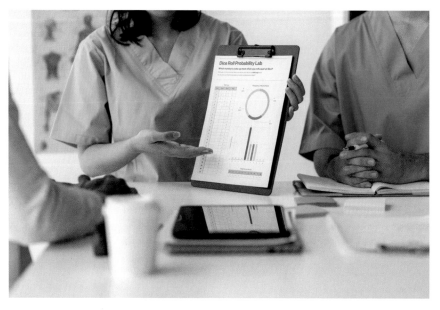

Despite the rapid pace of change and the novel disruptors in today's health care industry, Cleveland Clinic's chief strategy officer, Jim Cotelingam, says that many of the factors that hospitals and health systems want to consider in their strategic planning are not all that different from what has shaped planning in the past.

"I reviewed sample health system strategic plans from five and 10 years ago, and it struck me that many of the topics were quite similar to those in plans today," he notes. "Most of the topics are not truly novel, although some of the specific issues or concerns may have changed. For example, workforce issues may have been in previous plans, but the issue of violence faced by the workforce might be newer. But there is one noteworthy exception: artificial intelligence (AI). AI is just a game changer. I've seen it characterized as having the potential to disrupt human society the way the printing press did. And it has not been a major piece of any enterprise strategy I've worked on in the past."

How should health systems be thinking about AI in their strategic planning? "Because it is so relatively new but so incredibly powerful, it causes you to dream about what could be," Cotelingam says. "But it is important for health systems to focus on a five-year strategic plan by thinking about concrete ways in which they can apply AI and then going after those use cases."

As two examples, Cotelingam cites documentation and diagnostics. "Your plan could focus on leveraging AI tools in taking the burden off of providers by assisting with electronic health record (EHR) documentation or claims," he explains. "Payers are already saying that they are employing AI in claims processing. What could we be doing around documentation to help streamline the process? On the clinical side, consider specific areas of need like sepsis. Are there AI tools that can improve our ability to diagnose a case of sepsis earlier than usual? That would

About the Subject Matter Expert

As the chief strategy officer for Cleveland Clinic, **Jim Cotelingam** leads a team that is responsible for enterprise strategy development, major strategic initiative implementation, and strategic transactions such as mergers, acquisitions, and affiliations. Prior to joining Cleveland Clinic, he was the senior vice president of strategy for Trinity Health, one of the largest not-for-profit, faith-based health care systems in the nation. His career has given him unique insights into the forces that shape health system growth, and the strategic thinking necessary for success in an uncertain and constantly changing health care environment.

be of tremendous benefit to patients. In your planning process, don't wait for the perfect understanding of AI and the perfect roadmap to deploy it."

Unlike AI, cybersecurity is not a new area of focus in most hospitals' long-term strategic plans, but it has garnered more attention than ever before. A recent cyberattack on a payment cycle management company that affected the financial transactions of the vast majority of US hospitals is just one example of the stakes involved.

"Part of the reason you develop a strategic plan in the first place is to help you prioritize," Cotelingam says. "There are so many good things people want to do and so many needs in a community. But how can you pursue any of those goals if your information technology security is not there?" Change Health-care reportedly paid its attackers $22 million in ransom, so health care organizations are clearly lucrative targets. Cotelingam predicts that organizations can expect more of these attacks in the future and therefore must address cyber-security in their strategies.

Workforce Planning in an Increasingly Competitive Environment

Hospitals and health systems are accustomed to new entrants in the health care delivery space competing for both their patients and their providers, but the field is more crowded than ever. Private equity is bidding for specialists and primary care. Retailers such as Amazon, CVS, Walgreens, and Walmart are expanding their convenient, close-to-home medical offerings. Payers such as United and Optum are pursuing ultimate vertical integration.

"Workforce planning is more critical than ever," Cotelingam emphasizes. "You're no longer just competing with the hospital across the street when you're hiring physicians; you're competing with private equity or other nontraditional employers. Strategic planning needs to address where there might be gaps in supply and what new approaches your health system might need to consider to fill those gaps."

A complementary priority for hospital strategic planners should be the workforce environment, emphasizing systemic efforts to address burnout and stress, care for staff members' mental health, and manage increased threats of workplace violence.

Diversified Spaces and Novel Sources of Revenue

According to Cotelingam, the underlying economics of health care fundamentally differ among many parts of the country and many types of services.

"Growth that would have driven results on the bottom line in the past doesn't necessarily translate into the same results today," he says. "Health care systems cannot just rely upon the traditional set of services, delivered in the traditional way, to get the profitability they need to fund capital investment. Your strategic plan should reflect on market-specific spaces and how you want to play in those spaces. Where do you need to grow to create a sustainable enterprise, and how can you generate diversified sources of revenue and profitability?"

Cotelingam recommends that organizations think of markets in several contexts: by geography, by service line, and by payer. While pursuing a growth strategy, a health system should make sure that its strategic plan nurtures its existing markets.

"I have seen health systems get too far out over their skis and drain resources for existing markets while pursuing expansion into new ones," Cotelingam says. "Don't assume that those existing markets are on autopilot and don't need care and feeding. If you have strong competitors, that situation is even more acute. Capital is tight. While the stock market helped in 2023 with capital capacity, the operations of most health systems are still not at pre-pandemic levels, so it is a significant challenge to fund strategic growth while sustaining resources and investments for your base."

It is possible for hospitals and health systems to grow their systems but simultaneously erode their financial performance if the right strategic choices are not made. For organizations to continue serving their communities while choosing service lines and geographic regions that drive growth, they must recognize that they cannot be all things to all people in all locations.

"This means optimizing your footprint," Cotelingam says. "As you think about your strategic plan, you need alignment on what your highest-performing services and growth opportunities are at a granular level, not just broad categories like 'orthopedics.' Then you may need to concentrate some of those services in fewer locations by creating hubs to produce a better environment or higher quality, efficiency,

Health care executives from across the nation were asked how likely it is that the following will happen in their hospital or health system by 2030.

By 2030, our hospital or health system will have implemented clinical care AI support in at least two acute care service lines.

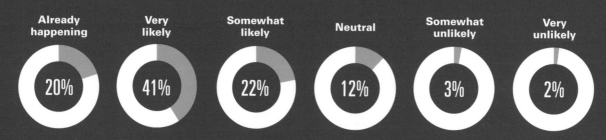

Already happening	Very likely	Somewhat likely	Neutral	Somewhat unlikely	Very unlikely
20%	41%	22%	12%	3%	2%

By 2030, the use of AI at our hospital or health system will have achieved 10 percent reduction in administrative costs (for example, because of task-oriented/workflow efficiencies and productivity).

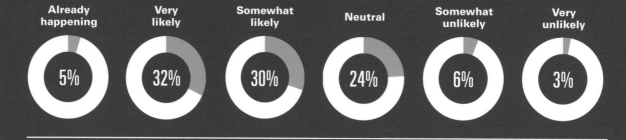

Already happening	Very likely	Somewhat likely	Neutral	Somewhat unlikely	Very unlikely
5%	32%	30%	24%	6%	3%

safety, and service. For example, in each of Cleveland Clinic's submarkets, we have identified a hub hospital that is going to do obstetrics and delivery. You cannot do this for everything, of course—primary care services need to be distributed to be close to people—but for something bigger, people will drive farther."

Cotelingam acknowledges that prioritization of geographic regions and services affects the culture of medical staff and requires tough decisions. "But that is part of the strategic planning process,"

he explains. "It should reveal the choices that need to be made in order to create economic sustainability."

Capacity Flexibility and Facility Planning

How do health systems plan for their footprint changes, given the drive toward the "hospital without walls," inpatient vs. outpatient care and lowest-cost sites of care? Cotelingam advises that organizations conduct a payer–product forecast and make sure that they have a good market-demand model.

"Ensure that you understand at a granular level what your utilization is and where you think it's going," he says. "One of the most impactful factors that can affect that model is traditional Medicare versus Medicare Advantage populations. If you have a larger population in unmanaged Medicare, your use rates will be higher, but as Medicare Advantage becomes more prominent in many parts of the country, we are seeing as much as 40 percent lower levels of utilization relative to traditional Medicare. The size of the facility you build and the capacity you need will vary greatly in these scenarios."

On the other hand, Medicare Advantage growth in an institution's area might prove to be a driver of *increased* patient demand, depending on its effects elsewhere in that institution's catchment area. "If it drives down excess inpatient utilization at smaller hospitals or weaker organizations, such that they have to reduce services or close entirely, that volume will have to go somewhere else," Cotelingam explains. "Here in Cleveland, three of our competitor hospitals have closed over the last couple of years, meaning that we and the other remaining hospitals are getting increased volume."

He suggests employing a Monte Carlo simulation as a highly effective tool for understanding the variability around these drivers of the market and their potential effect on patient demand or necessary facility capacity.

In uncertain times, Cotelingam also recommends investing in projects that have shorter payback periods, but he cautions against excessive pessimism about the future of traditional hospitals. "Even as we see absolutely inpatient surgical cases move to the outpatient side or be treated medically rather than surgically, we are also seeing an uptick in complex medical cases," he says. "I remember years ago when population health was supposed to take over the world, and a consulting firm published a paper predicting that inpatient utilization rates would decline by 30 percent. That did not happen. While I understand the perspective that inpatient care is declining—after all, I'm operating in a market where three hospitals have closed—hospitals are not going away, and those that remain will have an increasingly important role in their communities."

New Financial/ Reimbursement Models and Payment Reform

A health system's strategic plan must take into account the potential effects of new financial and reimbursement models and payment reform, such as

value-based care proposals from the Centers for Medicare and Medicaid Innovation (CMMI).

"The reality is that Medicare is becoming more and more dominant as a payer, and the Centers for Medicare and Medicaid Services ultimately want 100 percent of their members in value-based care arrangements," Cotelingam notes. "Surveys suggest that health system CEOs are skeptical about the benefit of some of the models put forward by CMMI over the years. However, given that only a fraction of those models produced the outcomes that they were looking for, value-based care is not going away. In the past, one payer wasn't dominant enough in many markets to have that kind of effect, but today, Medicare is so dominant enough that it can change markets."

You Can't Afford Not to Make Time for Strategy

Overall, according to Cotelingam, it is essential to pursue an integrated approach that unites strategic, financial, and capital planning rather than an isolated strategic plan.

"Your strategic plan must be directly linked to long-range financial forecasting, capital budgets, and operating budgets," he says. "Foundational to your strategy must be a shared understanding of the environment based on data and

analysis, and a shared point of view that synthesizes that data and analysis. Sometimes an institution will write an enterprise strategy, but the metrics that the team or the board use to manage the organization aren't directly tied to that enterprise strategy, so it creates a gap. At Cleveland Clinic, I have focused on ensuring that you can see the linkage between the metrics of organizational importance (what the board and the CEO think about and measure performance with), the work, and the strategy. It must be clear that the work and the strategy will help drive those metrics."

Cotelingam also notes that it is acceptable to sometimes leave strategies as broad visions that can be adapted to changing internal and external environments. These broad visions might be called "strategic focus areas." A five-year strategic plan does not have to be extremely detailed. It's more about changing mental models and making a commitment to those changes.

Still, it cannot sit on the shelf once it is complete. "I've been in environments where people write strategies for a hospital, and that's where it ends," Cotelingam says. "Who wants to spend time creating a strategic plan if it's not going to go anywhere? These plans are most meaningful when they are directly linked to market and service line plans and a capital plan that defines where you know you're going to grow, recapitalize, and make investments. They both interact with a multi-year financial plan, with all three influencing one another."

With so many pressures on hospitals and health systems to remain sustainable, one may wonder if there really is time to spare for the strategic planning process. Cotelingam argues that it is more important than ever: "In a constrained environment, understanding your priorities is absolutely essential. Having a strategic plan may not tell you how to do things better, but it can help confirm if you are doing the right things. I've worked with leaders who want to rush through the strategic planning process, jumping from 'We need to do a plan' to 'Here's the plan' with no steps in between. This is an area of responsibility for leaders and boards that it is worth taking the time to do right."

Key Takeaways

- **Workforce planning is crucial for health systems.** As a result, strategic planning should address potential gaps in labor supply and explore the new approaches a health system might need to consider to fill those gaps. The workforce environment is a complementary priority for hospital strategic planners. Systemic initiatives should address burnout and stress, caring for staff mental health, and managing increased threats of workplace violence.

- **Optimize your health system's footprint.** To choose service lines and geographies that drive growth while continuing to serve their communities, health systems need to realize that they cannot be all things to all people in all locations. Identify high-performing service lines and growth opportunities and consider concentrating those services in fewer locations by creating hubs to produce a better environment for quality, efficiency, safety, and service.

- **Health systems must pursue an integrated approach that unites strategic, financial, and capital planning.** This stands in contrast to an isolated strategic plan that isn't linked to long-range financial forecasting, capital budgets, or operating budgets. Foundational to any strategic plan must be a shared understanding of the environment that is based on data and analysis and a shared point of view that synthesizes those data and analysis.

The Survival of Small Organizations

with David Schreiner, PhD, FACHE, President/CEO, Katherine Shaw Bethea Hospital

Of the 6,120 hospitals in the United States, the vast majority—84 percent—are community hospitals. Of these, 32 percent—1,649 facilities—remain unaffiliated with any of the country's 400 integrated health systems (American Hospital Association 2024). How can these smaller organizations survive and even thrive in an increasingly competitive environment? According to David Schreiner, PhD, president and chief executive officer of Katherine Shaw Bethea Hospital (KSB) in Dixon, Illinois, being a smaller organization has its advantages. But the challenges are significant, especially in the wake of the pandemic.

The Current Health Care Landscape

"Small hospitals are still recovering from the impact of COVID-19 on their balance sheets," says Schreiner. KSB is an 80-bed facility serving a rural community of approximately 45,000 people. "Our day's cash on hand is at the point where capital investments are nearly impossible," he says. "We really can't invest in new wings or remodel a unit. It's a situation where we spend dollars on facilities or equipment only when we need to."

Generally, KSB sees a 2 to 3 percent annual increase in its net reimbursement. Expenses, however, have been rising in the double digits. "That's not a sustainable model, especially with 65 percent of our total expenses going toward compensation and benefits," Schreiner says. "The remaining 35 percent, our variable costs, provides the only opportunity to get our expense structure in line with our expected reimbursement."

Schreiner recommends that health care executives in smaller organizations consider where the organization needs to be in one year, three years, or five years: "If the conclusion is that the hospital will not be able to build that day's cash metric to a place where it can capitalize appropriately, then that could be a key tipping point for considering a partnership or affiliation."

In a large system, costs related to information technology (IT), legal counsel, human resources, purchasing/supply chains, and revenue cycle management are distributed among many hospitals, but independent hospitals

About the Subject Matter Expert

David L. Schreiner, PhD, FACHE, is president and CEO of Katherine Shaw Bethea Hospital (KSB) in Dixon, Illinois. He has served in various capacities at KSB for 35 years and has spent the last 13 years as CEO. Dr. Schreiner is a passionate advocate for rural hospitals and an inspiring and values-driven leader who strives every day to live up to his definition of leadership. His research focuses on improving executive communication. Dr. Schreiner was named the 2007 Dixon, Illinois, Citizen of the Year and received the 2022 Distinguished Alumni Award from the University of St. Francis College of Business. He is a past member of the board of governors of the American College of Healthcare Executives and the former chairman of the American Hospital Association Rural Health Task Force. He is the author of the best-selling book *Be the Best Part of Their Day: Supercharging Communication with Values-Driven Leadership*.

must cover such expenses entirely. In response to such heavy overhead, Schreiner has implemented some nontraditional strategies. "I've asked some managers to do double duty by supervising other departments, such as asking a pharmacist to also manage lab and X-ray. These are moves we're being forced to make as we try to lower our expenses to meet either declining reimbursement or a reimbursement rate that is rising much slower than our expenses are," he says. Fortunately, Schreiner has found partnerships on a small scale to be an option for enhancing the hospital's scope of services and cash flow. One partnership that has worked well is service line expansion.

"If we have a specialty or subspecialty that we are not able to offer in our community, it's been effective for us to find a physician from a health system to come into our community and spend one day a week or one day a month onsite," Schreiner notes. He says that many people in rural communities do not like to commute to urban areas. Bringing services to them through partnerships is a win-win for patients, the independent community hospital, and the provider who may not have previously had access to those patients. While partnerships are a way to structure these projects, this scenario could also trigger conversations on an affiliation between a health system and a hospital's leadership team.

"We're trying to play offense instead of defense because we are very close to having to cut as much as we can," Schreiner says. "Our strategy includes evaluating what services in our organization have a lower-than-expected market share and how we can address that. For instance, we haven't had an ear, nose, and throat specialist for a long time. We were able to hire an otolaryngologist and allied nurse practitioner, which almost instantly became a profitable service line for us. It also gives people in our service area the ability to receive that treatment locally as opposed to driving to Rockford or Chicago."

Other marketplace realities may trigger the exploration of a partnership or affiliation as well.

Recruitment and Retention

Recruitment and retention efforts could drive the need to consider an affiliation. "We initially think about needing physicians, of course, but there are also key positions such as pharmacists, nurse leaders, chief financial officers, IT specialists, and other difficult-to-recruit professionals," Schreiner states. "If your retention efforts are not working and you have limited success in recruitment, then you may eventually lose the ability to provide the services that are needed in your market."

Some candidates, however, find smaller hospitals attractive because they are independent. Decisions can be made locally, and these organizations are often more nimble than larger systems. "We have one gastroenterologist, and if he wants to add a new clinical offering, he doesn't have to take that through a series of committees and boards. Assuming that it is safe and in the best interest of patients, we can get that new procedure or service up and running in a matter of days," Schreiner says. He points out that for some staff members, there may be a risk of outmigration of talent once an affiliation is announced: "If a partnership is under consideration, health care executives may need to balance transparency with deferring an announcement of an affiliation until later in the due diligence process.

Payer Mix

Changes in a hospital's payer mix or the demographics of the community may put independent hospitals at risk of closure. "When we look at rural healthcare, the statistics are very clear in that these communities are getting older and sicker and that the education level is declining," Schreiner observes. "If a hospital's payer mix changes appreciably, even a few points can make a difference in the contribution to its margin." The impact on cash flow puts small organizations in a precarious situation. Schreiner notes that one hospital in his region had to close when a cyberattack prevented bills from getting out the door.

Local Competition

In cases where two independent hospitals operate in the same geographic area and one affiliates with a larger health system, the unaligned hospital experiences tremendous pressure. "They may have had similar income statements and balance sheets, but when one hospital gets a sudden infusion of cash, it may be able to grow faster and have a competitive edge, offering services it couldn't before," Schreiner notes. The fallout can be complex for unaffiliated competitors.

"On one level, there is the fear of being left out. The number of health systems is finite, and once they affiliate with one small hospital, they may not be interested in a second," Schreiner explains. "Of course, this doesn't mean that a merger is the right decision for your organization just because the hospital down the street has merged. Board members must prioritize doing what is best for their community and their local population. Organizations are not completely alike. That's why weighing all the factors is important: recruitment, degradation of the payor mix, executive team composition and vacancies, and increasingly heavy overhead."

Strategies for Health Care Leaders

Schreiner believes that health care leaders in small organizations may want to consider scaling back or eliminating services if cash flow has become a challenge. "Sometimes, eliminating services is the only choice. Take a close look at what's available locally. For instance, how many other home health care agencies are available in your service area? If there is a duplication of services, the hospital could potentially close that service and improve its margin." However, it is important to look at the downstream implications of closing a service. Schreiner estimates that his hospital would save about $640,000 a year if it were to close home care. "The challenge is what would happen to our readmission rate if those patients were not cared for in the same way that we care for them. What would happen to our length of stay if we had patients that we were unable to discharge because there were no services to safely care for them at home? The potential penalties for readmissions and the cost of keeping people in the hospital could actually surpass our savings."

Outsourcing is another option for selectively reducing personnel expenses. "Can we get smaller, maybe through attrition?" Schreiner asks. "Plant operations, dietary services, and housekeeping could be performed at less cost by an outside organization, which may be willing offer those positions to laid-off staff. We brought in an outside wound-care company, which hired all our

existing employees, and that service is now profitable."

In small nonprofit hospitals, it may take years to cultivate a donor base, but Schreiner believes the benefits are well worth the effort: "If your organization is fortunate enough to have a strong foundation, it can make a meaningful difference in helping to capitalize the organization."

Schreiner also suggests that health care executives explore ways to maximize reimbursement from payors. For example, organizations may consider negotiating better contracts, getting more favorable payment terms, or bringing in outside consultants with a fresh set of eyes. Schreiner points out that it is difficult for a single hospital to benchmark against itself.

Aside from the challenges of being a small hospital, KSB has a distinct advantage because of its local scale. "We know a lot of the people who enter our doors, and take pride in the way those patients and their families are treated," Schreiner declares. "Many rural and independent hospitals have outstanding patient engagement and employee engagement scores. I believe those two are linked. That is our secret sauce: that patients feel different when they come into our building and are treated differently than in other places. We take tremendous pride in that. I tell our employees all the time that in order for our organization to be successful, we have to give people a reason to stay in Dixon for health care when they could migrate to Rockford or Chicago. When patients go out of the community for one episode of care, we

may lose them for all of their health care needs."

Key Considerations

For a long time, KSB opted not to pursue affiliation with a health system. It had good reasons for doing so. "Our board is very aware of the history of the community and prides itself on being able to make decisions locally for patients who are their neighbors," Schreiner responds. "We are also one of the largest employers in our area. The loss of jobs is a real possibility during an acquisition. I heard of one hospital that had 800 employees pre-affiliation and perhaps 500 afterward. When you eliminate 300 jobs from a community of 50,000 people, that has a big impact on your neighbors."

When an affiliation becomes a viable possibility, Schreiner says it is critical to manage the expectations of the board of directors and the community. He has been educating his board for the last 10 years on mergers, affiliations, and partnerships. They have also seen the consequences when a community loses its hospital. "A medical center an hour away closed its doors, and we were the closest hospital for deliveries," he notes. "In that first year, we had 45 babies born at our hospital that would have otherwise been born there. Those moms had to drive an hour to deliver their baby, and that's not ideal."

Business leaders know that the closure of a hospital negatively affects not only the livelihoods of the employees who lost jobs but also leaders' ability to recruit executives and other workers

FUTURESCAN SURVEY RESULTS
Scale and Growth Opportunities

Health care executives from across the nation were asked how likely it is that the following will happen in their hospital or health system by 2030.

By 2030, our hospital or health system will enter a strategic partnership with a large health care system to achieve financial viability.

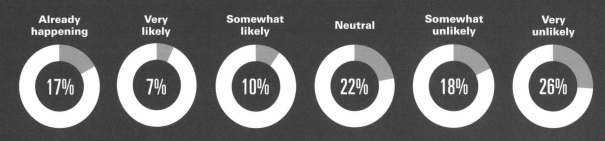

Already happening	Very likely	Somewhat likely	Neutral	Somewhat unlikely	Very unlikely
17%	7%	10%	22%	18%	26%

By 2030, our hospital will reduce its service lines in order to ensure financial viability.

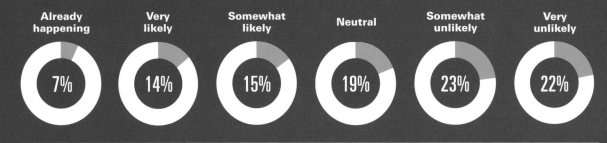

Already happening	Very likely	Somewhat likely	Neutral	Somewhat unlikely	Very unlikely
7%	14%	15%	19%	23%	22%

into local enterprises. Schreiner recommends that health care executives should inform their boards about strategies that are working and challenges that are present in the local environment. "It is important to talk about all the potential options, about board and community expectations, and about your mission and why you are there," he says. "Full transparency about the realities is essential."

In any discussion on long-term survival, it is important to include the national outlook on reimbursement by Medicare and Medicaid. According to the nonprofit Center for Healthcare Quality and Payment Reform, more

than 600 rural hospitals—nearly 30 percent of all rural hospitals—are at risk of closure in the near future. The median operating margin between July 2021 and June 2022 in rural hospitals was just 2.1 percent in states without Medicaid expansion and 3.99 percent in expansion states. Seven hospitals closed in 2022 (Levinson, Godwin, and Fuller 2023).

"I believe that there has to be meaningful reimbursement reform for small hospitals at the federal level," says Schreiner. "Even though critical access hospitals have the cost-plus reimbursement formula that is usually very favorable, a small hospital like mine has

been left out of the equation in many ways. We are what I refer to as tweener: a hospital that is positioned financially between the critical access hospitals and the academic medical centers. I don't think the current reimbursement model is going to be sustainable. The American Hospital Association is working very hard to find some potential new sources of reimbursement for rural hospitals and independent hospitals. I think we need to keep that sense of urgency at the in the front lines through our advocacy efforts if small hospitals are to survive."

Early in 2024, KSB finally made the decision to affiliate, applying the same thoughtfulness that had informed its earlier policy of nonaffiliation. The primary driver of the decision was KSB's inability to build sufficient financial reserves to invest capital into the plant and equipment. As a voting member of the board, Schreiner applauds the decision even as he recognizes the difficulty of the decision: "I have a tremendous amount of respect for the vision our members had in understanding what is in the best long-term interest of our community for the provision of health services."

Key Takeaways

As a health care executive who has maintained his organization's independence thus far but is now moving down the affiliation path and has also witnessed the aftermath of hospital and health system affiliations, Schreiner offers the following advice to other C-suite executives in smaller hospitals:

- **Know your community.** Schreiner believes that any partnership deliberations begin with knowing your community's "true north." What does your population need? Can you serve those needs in a more comprehensive way with independence or through an affiliation?
- **Educate the decision-makers.** Board members, medical staff, and the executive team all should understand the best way possible to take care of patients in the context of the hospital's mission. "Even though we may cherish the idea of doing that as an independent hospital, we can't afford to be blind to the fact that we may not be able to do as much if we remain independent," Schreiner notes.
- **Communicate.** "I cannot overemphasize the need for communication," says Schreiner. "We need to engage with the people who matter the most—our board members, business partners, physicians, and employees—and make sure that we listen to them and understand what their concerns are. At the same time, we need them to understand the challenges and environment we are facing."

Conclusion

While legislation to address the financial challenges of small rural community hospitals is moving through Congress, there are no guarantees that it will pass anytime soon. For Schreiner, that makes self-determination based on knowing your organization's true north even more essential. "Independent hospitals are very creative. We live among the people we serve, so we know better than anyone what our community needs. It's up to us to provide it, whether that's on our own or in an affiliation with a health system."

References

American Hospital Association. 2024. "Fast Facts on U.S. Hospitals, 2024." Updated January 12. https://www.aha.org/system/files/media/file/2024/01/fast-facts-on-us-hospitals-2024-20240112.pdf.

Center for Healthcare Quality & Payment Reform. 2024. "Rural Hospitals at Risk of Closing." Published July. https://ruralhospitals.chqpr.org/downloads/Rural_Hospitals_at_Risk_of_Closing.pdf.

Levinson, Z., J. Godwin, and S. Hulver. 2023. "Rural Hospitals Face Renewed Financial Challenges, Especially in States That Have Not Expanded Medicaid." KFF. Published February 23. https://www.kff.org/health-costs/issue-brief/rural-hospitals-face-renewed-financial-challenges-especially-in-states-that-have-not-expanded-medicaid/.

Behavioral Health's Digital Future

with Mike Rhoades, CEO of Alera Health

Digital platforms are among the most promising care delivery models for behavioral health services. Although the percentage of total health care expenditures devoted to behavioral health remains low at under 6 percent (Counts 2022), mental health conditions continue to affect the total cost of overall care in the United States. This reality is familiar to Mike Rhoades, chief executive officer of North Carolina–based Alera Health, which specializes in building integrated systems of care to support patients with primary/secondary behavioral health conditions. Rhoades calculates that behavioral health services account for over $188 billion in annual US health care expenditures while driving four times the amount of medical spending for patients suffering from co-occurring behavioral and chronic health conditions. In addition, hospitals write off over $18 billion in behavioral health related charity care.

The Current Health Care Landscape

"Hospitals and health systems that don't have access to a comprehensive network of inpatient and outpatient behavioral health services tend to see a real impact on their bottom lines from patients with behavioral health conditions," states Rhoades. In reviewing data on over 3 million patients, Alera Health

has calculated a hidden "behavioral health bed tax" of $10,000 to $15,000 per medical-surgical bed per year, which is attributable to the increased staff needed to manage these patients and the uncompensated care that is routinely written off as hospital charity care.

Rhoades explains that hospitals, and emergency room staff in particular, often feel overwhelmed by patients suffering from behavioral health conditions. "Hospital and primary care clinicians may feel inadequate in assessing behavioral health risks, which results in the decision to refer these patients to already-scarce inpatient psychiatric

beds to 'let them sort it out,'" he notes. "There is also confusion on how to navigate a multitude of psychiatric diagnostic conditions and a fragmented network of behavioral health services. In cases where psychiatric beds are limited or not available, medical-surgical hospitals end up boarding these patients, who may require an extra level of staffing and monitoring in a mixed-milieu environment. All of these factors make the cost of maintaining the status quo quite significant."

The need for behavioral healthcare is omnipresent. Mental Health America found the following information in its "State of Mental Health in America

About the Subject Matter Expert

Mike Rhoades is the CEO and founder of Alera Health, the largest manager of specialty behavioral health networks in the United States. Rhoades has over 30 years of experience in clinical and executive leadership in behavioral health, primary care, hospitals, and clinically integrated networks. Rhoades has expertise in network assemblage and governance, value-based contracting, population health technologies, data analysis, private equity, and public health/behavioral health policy. He has led over 20 merger and acquisition transactions and served in a variety of executive leadership roles.

2023" study (Reinert, Fritze, and Nguyen 2022):

- Over 50 million Americans—21 percent of the US population—are experiencing a mental illness.
- Fifteen percent of adults experienced a substance use disorder in 2020, and over 93 percent of them did not receive treatment.
- Fifty-five percent of adults with a mental illness—over 28 million people—receive no treatment.

Mental well-being is integral to physical health, and people with behavioral health conditions such as depression and substance use disorders are at greater risk of developing chronic diseases. Additionally, behavioral health disorders significantly aggravate chronic health outcomes. "If your organization participates in an accountable care organization or operates a provider-led health plan, behavioral health inflates total medical costs for patients with at least one chronic medical condition by a factor of 3.5 to 4," Rhoades says. Linking patients with the mental health services they need is becoming essential as reimbursement moves toward value-based care.

The paradox is that patients with more severe mental health disorders are frequently the most difficult to engage in treatment. "These are often the patients with the biggest spend profile," says Rhoades. "They also typically score the worst on their HEDIS metrics. That makes this population the biggest opportunity in lowering total cost of care."

Nationwide, the use of telehealth for accessing both medical and behavioral health services increased dramatically during the pandemic. In 2023, the highest utilization of telehealth was for accessing mental health services, with 37 percent of patients using it for that purpose (Bartelt et al. 2023). However, digital health includes a plethora of solutions beyond telehealth, including mobile apps, remote monitoring, and wearables.

"There is a lot of conversation around deploying digital health solutions in behavioral health, but this comes with

clinical and business risks that deserve careful and thoughtful study," says Rhoades. "I don't believe that we will see digital health replace a human connection anytime soon. However, digital solutions within the behavioral health space will absolutely augment care by helping to monitor and engage patients in the white space between patient/clinician interactions."

Strategies for Health Care Leaders

Rhoades suggests that as providers venture further into value-based care, they will need to emphasize more convenient and accessible care to their patients. For example, using care coordination referral and communication tools can help integrate a multi-specialty care team so that patients only have to tell their story once. By integrating referral and communication tools with real-time teleconsultation, these technologies can create a virtual hub-and-spoke model where a "walk-in multi-specialty clinic" can incorporate real-time integrated health data to provide treatment, enable on-demand screenings, close care gaps, and receive specialty e-consultations. These techniques conveniently make the visit a "one-stop shop" rather than a series of follow-up appointments, which can be challenging for a patient with social and financial obstacles to care (such as transportation or childcare needs). Rhoades believes that functionality such

as e-referrals, care navigation, clinical data exchanges, secure messaging, and real-time care alerting in an actionable format empower a patient's care team to become proactive and prevent avoidable, costly care events.

Another useful feature of digital health is to act as a force multiplier for expensive and hard-to-recruit staff. "Not every specialty provider can be physically located in a single place. On-demand telehealth can fill in those gaps," Rhoades states. For hospitals and health systems that do not have their own behavioral health infrastructure, digital health tools that operationalize partnerships with specialty providers of behavioral health can be much more scalable and often better for the community. These collaborations can also result in downstream cost efficiencies and can streamline care coordination.

Digital Health Solutions at Major Health Systems

Lifebridge Health is a five-hospital acute care system in Maryland that has a full continuum of behavioral health services in place. These services include one adult and two child/adolescent inpatient units, a partial-hospitalization program for adults, two large mental health outpatient clinics, two addiction recovery programs, and psychiatric emergency teams that respond to crises out in the community. With a shortage of qualified behavioral health professionals in the Baltimore market, Lifebridge is using digital health to expand its staff and manage the demand for emergency assessments and for individual and group therapy.

"We have a team of licensed clinical social workers in Israel who are available virtually to conduct emergency safety assessments during hard-to-fill nighttime hours," says Dawn Hurley, vice president of behavioral health at Lifebridge. "They are licensed to practice in the state of Maryland."

Lifebridge therapists also routinely conduct individual and group therapy using a secure mobile platform, and the same technology is used when needs arise on inpatient units at any of its five medical centers. "Mental health is the number-one concern at each of our hospitals and has been since COVID," Hurley says. The system is in the early phase of embedding licensed clinical social workers (LCSWs), or the linkage to an on-demand LCSW, within primary care practices. Lifebridge is participating in a larger, grant-funded effort within the central Maryland area to provide 24-hour mobile crisis intervention service that will offer same-day or next-day virtual visits.

In order to better reach patients who need behavioral health services, some health systems are adding patient-facing features and content that can be integrated into their online portals or mobile apps. The easiest and most productive tactic is to incorporate behavioral health awareness and wellness campaigns into all forms of organizational communications, including digital health. An added bonus of digital health solutions, according to Rhoades, is how they can connect hospitals and behavioral health providers with patients in ways that create a "sticky" and expandable relationship between the health system and the patient. "A patient-facing mobile app that offers a singular portal to conduct several care functions is going to be utilized more than a point solution for a specific task," he states.

Rather than building these solutions from scratch, health systems may consider partnerships with digital health

companies willing to customize their existing technology in exchange for a brand relationship and/or data that can be used to refine the toolset. While most health systems may eventually want to integrate a digital health solution into their electronic health records (EHRs), Rhoades emphasizes the importance of not letting EHR integration stifle innovation. A great deal of technology may fit better outside the EHR or as part of a health system's population health management tools.

"For now and into the foreseeable future, I am more interested in practical digital solutions that make scheduling easier, digitize phone and fax communications, convert big data into actionable alerts, improve risk stratification and forecasting, and automate wellness checks," Rhoades says. "These operational tasks may be less exciting than an 'avatar therapist,' but they represent significant administrative waste and friction in the care delivery system that could be re-invested in treatment and services."

With the digital health field still in its infancy, some limitations have yet to be addressed. "Some of the technology requires changes in the user's behavior," notes Rhoades. "Are providers and patients ready to adopt and adapt to the technology?" There is also the issue of interoperability among information technology platforms. When deciding whose platform will prevail, this is less a

technical problem than a political one. It will be critical for hospitals and health systems to have their existing and future value-based agreements reward the initiative monetarily over multiple years to facilitate a return on investment.

Brick-and-mortar facilities still have a place. About 70 percent of behavioral health visits are conducted face-to-face, and the trend is toward more behavioral healthcare being delivered via community outreach and home visits to engage patients who don't readily show up for appointments. Luckily, community outreach is not a new delivery concept for behavioral health providers, which have been conducting community-based care for over 40 years out of necessity to find and engage behavioral health patients. Rhoades says, "They know where to find patients, how to establish rapport with patients and conduct field assessments, and how to convert a motivational interview into patient activation." Digital tools can be a valuable asset in automating routine research, streamlining documentation, and electronically coordinating follow-up care in a manner that allows higher caseloads without sacrificing efficacy.

Alera Health's use of digital tools demonstrates just how valuable such assets can be. Alera has established partnerships with health systems like Banner Health, a $14 billion health system operating 30 acute care hospitals across six states, an insurance division, and an accountable care organization with 1.2 million lives. The goal is to address the prevalence of mental health conditions in defined patient populations and to mitigate the total cost of care and the financial impact on the hospital. Both organizations have integrated various referral and data systems in a manner that does not require one party to abandon its technology and workflow in favor of another.

In 2023, Banner University Health Plan contracted with Integral Health Network of Southern Arizona (IHNSA), a multi-specialty behavioral health network managed by Alera Health, to manage the medical and behavioral health care for over 9,000 Medicaid members. IHNSA acts as "quarterback" for the roughly 10 percent of Banner Health patients who struggle, because of ongoing behavioral health issues, to engage and follow up in their health care, resulting in eight times more emergency department visits and a total cost of care exceeding $2,500 per member per month.

IHNSA's responsibilities included outreach to members, many of whom did not have current phone numbers and addresses; whole health assessments; development of a care plan; scheduling of appointments, including home and community-based care; transitional

support between levels of care; and mitigation of social determinants of health issues that impede care engagement. To automate certain care coordination tasks, both IHNSA and Banner Health use Alera's *Care Optimization System*, which pushes real-time care and gap alerts into a shared platform for e-referrals, communication, and care management. This platform includes a patient-facing mobile app to support scheduling, transportation, disease literacy, telehealth, and wellness checks. This public utility is free to use for any member of a patient's care team and can both operate as a stand-alone system and integrate into various EHRs.

In 2023 IHNSA and its sister network, Affiliated Network Providers (both leveraging the Alera Health ONEcare model), increased patient engagement and closed care gaps, which resulted in a 9.1 percent reduction in total cost of care and approximately $75 million in savings. ONEcare Networks positively affected patient care in many other ways, as shown in exhibit 1.

Collaboration between hospitals and health systems and their digital health partners appears to be a viable possibility. In the spring 2024 *Futurescan* survey, 57 percent of respondents said that partnering with digital behavioral health providers to deliver care was "very

likely" or "somewhat likely" to occur for their organizations in the next five years. Fifty-two percent said it was "very likely" or "somewhat likely" that their organization will have doubled their capacity for treating behavioral health with digital solutions over the same period of time.

Important Financial Considerations

Strategies for maximizing reimbursement for digital health solutions are still evolving but often do not keep pace with the technology. While some CPT codes are related to monitoring certain digital health outputs, there is little in the way of reimbursement for the technology itself.

"That may initially be discouraging, but health care leaders should weigh the secondary and tertiary benefits of lower labor costs, enhanced relationships with patients and other providers, and improved health outcomes that can translate into value-based incentives," Rhoades says. "For behavioral health, I don't see a movement to reimburse for digital tools happening anytime soon. But I do believe there will be indirect rewards for the use of such tools through value-based incentives. Payers are likely to let the provider market sift through the digital health marketplace to identify

Exhibit 1

Effects of ONEcare Networks on Patient Care

269	Additional patients (+14%) maintained compliance with their Depression Medication for 80% of the year
57%	Of patients discharged from a psychiatric hospitalization engaged in aftercare within 7 days (20% improvement)
51%	Of all patients discharged from an emergency department (ED) following a mental health visit engaged in aftercare within 7 days (48% improvement)
1,338	Additional patients (+31%) received a Breast Cancer Screening this year over last
2,558	Additional members (+24%) received a cervical cancer screening this year over last
1,483	More kids and teenagers (+68%) received a well care visit
78%	Of pregnant mothers received prenatal care (48% improvement)
1,108	Fewer (–31%) ED visits by attributed patients in 2023

Source: Used by permission of Alera Health.

FUTURESCAN SURVEY RESULTS
Behavioral Health

Health care executives from across the nation were asked how likely it is that the following will happen in their hospital or health system by 2030.

By 2030, our hospital or health system will have doubled its capacity for treating behavioral health with digital solutions.

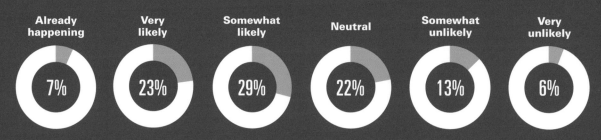

Already happening	Very likely	Somewhat likely	Neutral	Somewhat unlikely	Very unlikely
7%	23%	29%	22%	13%	6%

By 2030, our hospital or health system will collaborate with digital behavioral health partners in order to deliver care.

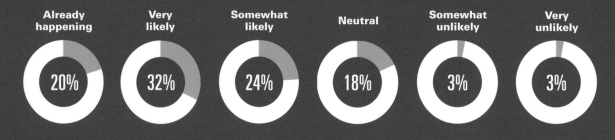

Already happening	Very likely	Somewhat likely	Neutral	Somewhat unlikely	Very unlikely
20%	32%	24%	18%	3%	3%

for themselves which technologies generate the highest return on investment."

Key Takeaways
Rhoades suggests the following three takeaways for health care leaders who want to add or expand behavioral health services through digital technology.

- Clarify the problems you want to solve. Is your emergency room being overwhelmed by patients in crisis, with no clear pathway for triaging them? Is your organization's bottom line strained by patients with mental health issues and accompanying comorbidities that are unchecked because of noncompliance with treatment plans? "From there, you can set forth your strategic vision and expectations for how digital health can help achieve those goals," Rhoades says. "Technology is becoming cheaper to build than to deploy, so it pays to build the tech around your needs rather than morphing your organization to off-the-shelf technology."

- Assemble a comprehensive behavioral health network by either hiring your own complement of providers or partnering with an aggregator who can assemble multi-specialty behavioral health organizations. "Keep in mind that behavioral health is not a singular disorder but rather a compendium of over 3,000 different diseases," Rhoades states, "Once the services are in place, look for digital methods to facilitate communication, care coordination, data sharing and analytics so that patients only have to tell their story once as they move through the system of care."

- Understand the patient/provider experience and their requirements to ensure technology adoption and engagement. "Forcing a new technology on the user often results in 'tech-sclerosis,' wherein the user refuses to adopt or attempts work-arounds. When the platform is perceived as valuable by the customer, brand loyalty and stickiness is enhanced."

Conclusion

Rhoades believes that over the next five years, access to behavioral health will improve and thus encourage the medical community to conduct more screenings to identify those silent sufferers. "Not every behavioral health event may require professional treatment, but no behavioral health condition has ever been cured through shame," he says. "From mobile apps to patient portals, these technologies can make pursuing treatment seem mainstream."

For organizations partially or fully committed to value-based care, digital behavioral health platforms can help reduce the overall cost of care and improve patient outcomes. They can also help strengthen the provider-patient connection. "If you believe, as I still do, that there will always be a human in human services, then search for digital tools that magnify the impact of your care team."

References

Bartelt, K., A. Piff, S. Allen, and E. Barkley. 2023. "Telehealth Utilization Higher Than Pre-Pandemic Levels, but Down from Pandemic Highs." Epic Research. Published November 21. https://www.epicresearch.org/articles/telehealth-utilization-higher-than-pre-pandemic-levels-but-down-from-pandemic-highs.

Counts, N. 2022. "Behavioral Health Care in the United States: How It Works and Where It Falls Short." Commonwealth Fund. Published September 7. https://doi.org/10.26099/txpy-va34.

Reinert, M., D. Fritze, and T. Nguyen. 2022. "The State of Mental Health in America 2023." Mental Health America. Published October. https://mhanational.org/sites/default/files/2023-State-of-Mental-Health-in-America-Report.pdf.

All-Payer Total Cost of Care Models

with Tori Bayless, CEO of Luminis Health

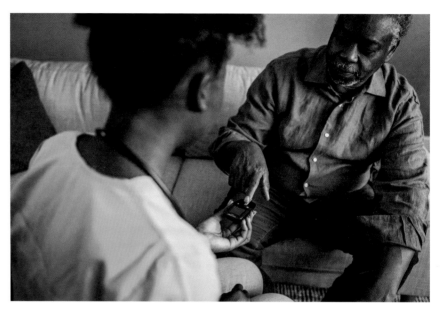

In the fall of 2023, the Centers for Medicare & Medicaid Services (CMS) announced a new, voluntary total cost of care (TCOC) alternative payment model. The States Advancing All-Payer Health Equity Approaches and Development (AHEAD) model aims to lower the rate of growth in health care spending while improving population health and reducing disparities in care and access. Under AHEAD, participating hospitals would receive a global budget for inpatient and outpatient departments that supported a predefined population of patients. States participating in AHEAD are accountable for quality and population health outcomes, and the program reduces all-payer avoidable health care spending to encourage statewide and regional health care transformation. Although these payments are for traditional Medicare and Medicaid, other payers may also participate. In fact, at least one commercial payer must participate in each state. Up to eight states will be selected to participate in this 11-year pilot program. The first cohort of participating states include Maryland, Vermont, and Connecticut, with Hawaii anticipated to follow. Cohort 3 applications were due August 12.

What are the prospects for the success of AHEAD, one of the latest in a series of innovation models from the Center for Medicare and Medicaid Innovation (CMMI) that are aimed at improving population health and lowering costs? Some insights are available from Maryland, one of the primary models for AHEAD, which has had evolving forms of an all-payer system since the mid-1970s. Maryland's system—which has developed from unit rates through a "charge-per-case" structure and a hospital per capita model—has developed over the past several decades, ultimately leading into today's TCOC system.

Tori Bayless, chief executive officer (CEO) of Maryland-based Luminis Health, is well acquainted with these dimensions of health care in her state.

"The federal government has evaluated Maryland's model over the past 10 years and has seen its success in bending the cost curve," she says.

How did Maryland get to this point, and what lessons can the Maryland experience offer to improve AHEAD's chances of success?

The Maryland Model

In the early 1970s, the state health care payment system in Maryland was a national example—and not in a good way. Plagued by inefficiencies and overutilization, with excess capacity and hospital lengths of stay that exceeded the national average, the average hospital cost per case exceeded the national average by more than 25 percent.

In 1971, Maryland's General Assembly created the Health Services Cost Review Commission (HSCRC), an independent body within the state's Department of Health and Mental Hygiene. The General Assembly gave HSCRC the authority to establish hospital- and service-specific rates for all inpatient, hospital-based outpatient and emergency services.

The HSCRC's mandate was to ensure fair, equitable, and predictable rates for all payers; maximize access to care; contain hospital costs; and provide public accountability. After a three-year phase-in, the HSCRC officially began setting rates in 1974. In 1977, Maryland was granted a temporary waiver by the federal government to test alternative hospital payment approaches, which exempted it from the Inpatient Prospective Payment System and Outpatient Prospective Payment System and allowed Maryland to set its own rates for these services, with all third parties paying the same rate.

Bending the Cost Curve: How TCOC Has Worked in Maryland

It took some time for the TCOC model to mature. In 1976, the year before the Medicare waiver was put in place, the state's cost per case was still a dismal 25 percent higher than the national average. However, that difference began dropping dramatically in 1981. By 1984, Maryland's cost per case was a scant 2 percent higher than the national average and was never above the national average again. By 1992, total cost per case was 12 percent *below* the national average.

Those gains were jeopardized in the 2000s, as changes in the health care delivery system eroded Maryland's "waiver cushion." "There were cost increases not adequately reflected in the system, including staffing costs," Bayless explains. As a result, Maryland was granted a new all-payer model by CMMI, which launched in January 2014. All hospitals shifted from a rate regulation all-payer system to global budgets.

"In one fell swoop, all of Maryland's hospitals moved to global budgets," Bayless notes. "The incentive was to shift from volume to value, to keep people out of the hospital and get them the care they need in lower-cost settings. There is a lot of transparency: Everyone sees everyone else's data and can learn from one another." From 2014 to 2018, Maryland hospitals generated over $975 million in savings operating under global budgets and demonstrated improvements in inpatient admissions, potentially avoidable hospitalizations, and mortality.

In 2019, building on lessons from these previous iterations of the all-payer model, the state adopted an even more ambitious version: TCOC, which establishes pricing of medical services provided by hospitals and sets growth targets across all payers. This set Maryland on course to achieve defined savings to Medicare for the TCOC each year between 2019 and 2023 for a total of over $1 billion in Medicare TCOC savings by the fifth year.

"Not only did global budgets persist, but hospitals also were made responsible for the cost of care for *all* Medicare beneficiaries in their defined service areas," Bayless says. Part of the challenge in many TCOC models, including the Maryland model, is identifying appropriate methods for attribution, Bayless says: "This is very tricky because people

are not 'assigned' to any particular health system." This often means that the hospital or health system may control only a portion of the care received but must serve as the convener for all providers—physicians, post-acute care, ambulatory surgery, labs, and imaging centers—in an effort to control the entire cost of care for Medicare beneficiaries.

Under TCOC, global budgets and quality programs came together. "We implemented quality incentives around numerous factors, including readmission rates, timely follow-up for chronic conditions, infection rates, mortality rates, and the patient experience," Bayless says. "These are just some of the elements incorporated into the quality-based reimbursement, for all patients and all payers. As the model evolved, we also increased our focus on disparity measures and health equity."

Rural and safety-net hospitals can also benefit from the stability and predictability that global budgets and TCOC payment models provide. "The big principles of the model are cost, quality, and access—and those stabilize rural and inner-city safety net hospitals," Bayless explains. "There are several rural and urban hospitals that would have closed without this structure."

In 2019, the first performance year of the model, Maryland reduced TCOC spending relative to national trends by $365 million (see exhibit 1).

Exhibit 1

Annual Savings of Maryland TCOC

Year	Target Savings	Actual Cost Savings
2019	$120 million	$364.85 million
2020	$156 million	$390.6 million
2021	$222 million	$378.1 million
2022	$267 million	$269 million

Source: Data from HSCRC (2023).

The model was scheduled to conclude at the end of 2023, but with CMMI interested in establishing more uniformity in their models nationwide, the agency granted Maryland an extension to determine a future model.

Maryland as an Early Adopter for AHEAD

In the AHEAD model, participating states assume responsibility for managing health care quality and costs across payers, including Medicare, Medicaid, and at least one private payer. According to CMS, states also assume responsibility for ensuring that health providers in their state deliver high-quality care, improve population health, offer greater care coordination, and advance health equity by supporting underserved patients.

"Through AHEAD, CMS aims to strengthen primary care, improve care coordination, and increase screening and referrals to community resources like housing and transportation to address social drivers of health," notes CMS's overview of the model (CMS 2023a). CMS added that AHEAD will provide participating states with funding and other tools to address rising health care costs and support health equity: "AHEAD aims to increase resources available to participating states to improve the overall health of their population, support primary care, and transform health care in their communities" (CMS 2023b).

While the concept of TCOC holds promise, as demonstrated by the Maryland model, design features and expectations must be adapted to account for post-COVID realities and for states that may not have the same infrastructure and experience that Maryland has developed over the last several decades. "Workforce scarcity, supply chain defects, skyrocketing drug costs, payer denials, and underfunded inflation have strained hospitals' financial performance and ability to reinvest," notes Bayless. Resources to support infrastructure investment will be necessary for AHEAD to be successful.

There is also some concern about the effects of the TCOC model on system growth. Growth caps and service line adjustments could disincentivize expansion. "If you're growing, you're making less money, and if you're shrinking, you're making more. That defies typical market dynamics and business principles," Bayless says. "Incentives are aligned to drive care to lower-cost settings. The risk is that, as more and more care is provided outside hospitals, hospitals are left with very expensive physical plants and technology they may not be able to maintain." Observing that hospitals have always been able to provide a robust complement of services that cross-subsidize one another, Bayless continues, "With lower-acuity care moving outside of hospitals, those hospitals could be at risk of becoming safety-net intensive care units."

Other potential drawbacks of rate-setting models include the potential for underpayment. "A hospital or health system could get stuck in a rate regulation system in which it is set to be paid X but the costs escalate to X plus Y," Bayless says. "We saw some of that in Maryland during the pandemic, when costs were going up much faster than the HSCRC reimbursement rates were."

This means that without appropriate adjustments, TCOC models may not solve reimbursement inadequacies that are also present under fee-for-service arrangements.

Other States' Experience With Rate-Setting Models

Bayless notes that some states have had challenging experiences with rate-setting models. "New York and New Jersey, for example, pursued all-payer rate-setting models in the 1980s, but they ultimately walked away for a number of reasons, while Maryland's model persisted," Bayless says.

What sets Maryland apart? One advantage, Bayless acknowledges, is extra funding from Medicare: "In our 'all-payer' system, Medicare pays more for hospital care than it does in other states, and commercial payers pay less," she explains. "In other states, for example, Medicare pays a dollar for every $1.50 that commercial payers lay out, while in Maryland it's the same rate for all payers. This prevents cost shift to commercial insurers that occurs in the rest of the country. As such, commercial payers benefit financially and support the model."

How could AHEAD make that work in a larger multistate pilot? Medicare needs to create sufficient financial incentive in the program; otherwise, Bayless predicts, the AHEAD model may face resistance. "If you're in a growth mode—advancing health care access to patients in your communities and investing in facilities, clinical programs and physician recruitment—a global budget could slam the brakes on those investments," she notes. The ultimate tension, of course, is that hospitals need more money, and payers don't want to be responsible for paying it. "There is a lot of transparency around what hospitals are paid and our costs and margins," Bayless continues. "Meanwhile, premiums in the insurance world have been increasing two to three times what hospital rates are, and yet the payers haven't had that same level of transparency. Even here in Maryland, there is not enough attention to or transparency around what is and is not allowed for payers."

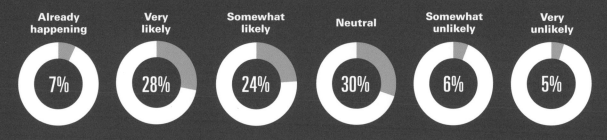
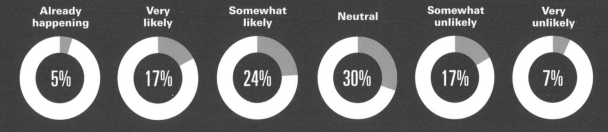
Top Three Takeaways: How Should Health Systems Prepare?

In states that elect to pursue the AHEAD model, how should health systems prepare?

- **Pace yourself and understand what you already have.** "Be thoughtful about the amount of change you're about to face," Bayless says. "AHEAD involves global budgets, care transformation, primary care, health equity, and a focus on total cost of care for Medicare beneficiaries. That's not dramatically different from what many health systems are already doing in terms of diversified networks, ambulatory facilities, and partnerships with post-acute providers."

- **Adjust to a new paradigm where you are responsible for what you do not control.** If an institution has been focused on growing volumes and market share, Bayless cautions that AHEAD will require a different point of view in which health systems are responsible for the TCOC even for elements they do not control. "You will need to broaden your focus to keeping people out of the hospital, managing chronic illness, and reducing costs, while partnering more effectively with the post-acute environment," she suggests. "Even if you don't control all the elements of the delivery system for Medicare beneficiaries, you do influence many of them." This also applies to ramping up care management and care navigation to ensure that the highest-risk patients have the right wraparound services they need: "The hospital doesn't have to build all of them, but they do need to coordinate supportive partnerships around food insecurity, transportation, and making sure that populations with significant needs are able to keep appointments and get their prescriptions filled," Bayless notes. "One question is how do you link up those services."

- **Build in shared accountability and evaluation.** When health systems take on responsibility under the AHEAD model, they must plan for some level of shared accountability and decision-making, Bayless advises. "You need a governance structure from the beginning, involving a council of stakeholders including payers, providers, representatives from the state department of health, and elected officials." Evaluation of these programs and processes should also be built in from the beginning, she concludes. "You need to decide on your KPIs from the front end, and what you expect to learn from those. Policies, rate methodologies, and quality incentives may be well intentioned and may work in the early stages, but they will likely require revision and updating going forward. You need the flexibility

to assess what is working and what is not."

Conclusion

While the AHEAD model is scheduled for implementation in 2026, it will be crucial to learn from the experiences in states that have pursued other TCOC models. Pennsylvania and Vermont have also had previous TCOC models (the Pennsylvania Rural Health Model and Vermont All Payer ACO Model). If AHEAD is to succeed in additional states, Bayless believes it will need regulatory authority similar to Maryland's HSCRC. "Maryland's HSCRC was created to work on behalf of Marylanders to ensure that we are balancing cost, quality, and access and are operating within the confines of the contract the state has with the federal government under the Medicare waiver and the TCOC model," she says. "To develop a similar model, you can't just snap your fingers. You need a layer of regulatory authority to provide the infrastructure for oversight and successful implementation."

References

Centers for Medicare & Medicaid Services (CMS). 2023a. "CMS Announces Transformative Model to Give States Incentives and Flexibilities to Redesign Health Care Delivery, Improve Equitable Access to Care." Published September 5. https://cms.gov/newsroom/press-releases/cms-announces-transformative-model-give-states-incentives-and -flexibilities-redesign-health-care.

———. 2023b. "States Advancing All-Payer Health Equity Approaches and Development (AHEAD) Model." Published September 20. https://cms.gov/priorities/innovation/innovation-models/ahead.

Health Services Cost Review Commission (HSCRC). 2023. "CY 2022 Total Cost of Care Performance Letter." Published September 20. https://hscrc.maryland.gov/Documents/Modernization/Model%20Documents/2022%20TCOC%20 Performance%20Letter%20and%20Cover%20Letter%20with%20Signatures.pdf.

5 VALUE-BASED CARE DISRUPTION

Disruption in the Era of Value-Based Care

with Barry Arbuckle, PhD, President/CEO, MemorialCare

The concept of value-based care as an alternative to traditional fee-for-service reimbursement has existed for well over a decade. Value-based care, also known as accountable care, received unequivocal validation as the preferred payment model when the Centers for Medicare and Medicaid (CMS) established the CMS Innovation Center in 2010 to identify ways to improve health care quality and reduce costs in government-funded health care programs. Since then, there has been an acceleration in the shift from a health care system that pays for volume to one that pays for value. A value-based contract in health care is an agreement between health care providers and payers that ties reimbursement levels to the quality and outcomes of care provided rather than to the volume of services delivered. These contracts aim to improve patient outcomes and reduce overall healthcare costs by incentivizing providers to focus on delivering high-quality, efficient care. But the adoption of the value-based care model has been relatively slow, as CMS and commercial payers continue to reimburse under the more lucrative fee-

for-service arrangement that rewards the provision of more—not fewer—services.

According to Barry Arbuckle, president and chief executive officer of Southern California–based Memorial-Care, the leading development so far in the adoption of accountable care has been the growth in Medicare Advantage plans. "CMS is really leaning into value-based care and trying to move both Medicare and Medicaid providers to

adopt these payment models," he says. "Those efforts have resulted in Medicare Advantage becoming the predominant payment model for seniors rather than traditional Medicare, with more than 50 percent enrollment across the country."

CMS intends to move all traditional Medicare beneficiaries into a value-based care model by 2030. Most health plans have introduced some form of a

---

About the Subject Matter Expert

Barry Arbuckle, PhD, is president and CEO of MemorialCare, a leading nonprofit integrated health system with three adult hospitals, one children's hospital, and more than 230 outpatient care sites throughout Southern California. A committed advocate for health care reform, Arbuckle was one of three California health system executives recently selected to serve on the advisory committee for the California Office of Health Care Affordability. He also serves on the executive committee and the board of directors of the Healthcare Leadership Council and as a member of the Health System Executive Council

of the Bipartisan Policy Center, both national organizations headquartered in Washington, DC. Arbuckle is a former chair of the Integrated Healthcare Association and the California Hospital Association.

Arbuckle serves on Becker's Healthcare National Advisory Board and is a sought-after speaker nationally and globally on a variety of health care topics, including health system strategy, innovation, partnerships, ambulatory care strategies, behavioral health, and value-based contracting with health plans and employers.

value-based plan, but the adoption has been slow overall. In 2022, 36 percent of the lives in commercial, Medicare Advantage, Medicaid, or traditional Medicare plans were covered by accountable care arrangements (Health Care Payment Learning & Action Network 2023).

Transforming a Health System Around Value-Based Care

MemorialCare began developing the supporting infrastructure for the provision of value-based care in 2014. The health system comprises four hospitals and over 250 sites of care, including over 100 community-based ambulatory centers that are built intentionally around value-based care. The model focuses on lowering costs and improving outcomes, goals that MemorialCare has embraced on a large scale.

"Value-based care focuses on doing procedures at the right site of care both clinically and financially—for the patient," Arbuckle states. Memorial-Care has entered into joint ventures with imaging centers, ambulatory care sites, and surgery centers, where many of the diagnostic tests and procedures that could be provided in a hospital outpatient center are performed in a less costly community setting. Many health care leaders would find this model disruptive for their own organizations. "We have passed up millions of dollars in reimbursement to do what we believe is right and forward-looking. We intentionally move patients to places because they are the right sites of care, even though our reimbursement is lower. It is an unusual way to go about business, but we are incentivized to lower costs and improve quality and access though our contractual relationships."

MemorialCare's primary care providers proactively reach out to patients before they need a medical visit. "We want them to have the preventive screenings they need and the education that will keep them healthy," Arbuckle explains. "When a health system is at financial risk for the medical care of an entire population, it's critical to increase the number and kinds of access points along the continuum of care."

To respond to this reality, Memorial-Care has built an extensive portfolio of digital and virtual care assets in addition to its robust and growing ambulatory network. For instance, virtual urgent care is available around the clock, 365 days a year. During visits over the web, patients type in their symptoms, and artificial intelligence is used asynchronously to determine the level of care they might need. A chatbot then links them to a provider, who responds within an hour. The system also offers e-consultations and remote patient monitoring. "The bottom line is that digital access is important to consumers who are accustomed to doing everything on their phones," Arbuckle notes.

To deliver on this expectation, the health system has developed a MemorialCare app that integrates with the MyChart patient portal and enables users to schedule in-person or virtual visits and behavioral health sessions, view test results, communicate with providers, and more. "Value-based care works best when it circumvents health issues before they get more serious," Arbuckle says. "Many patients are unsure whether they need an emergency room (ER) visit or urgent care—and 30 to 40 percent of the time, the ER is not the right place to go."

Another cost-cutting initiative has involved embedding behavioral health providers in primary care clinics. "We know the financial impact that

immediately addressing behavioral health issues can have on medical expenditures," Arbuckle says. "Primary care providers (PCPs) are not routinely trained to assess depression, anxiety, bipolar disorder, or schizophrenia. In this model, PCPs can immediately hand off a patient to a behavioral health provider. It yields better outcomes, but there is a significant expense. Again, we're spending money to get paid less. But it irrefutably lowers the cost of care while maintaining or improving quality and access."

MemorialCare established California's first direct-to-employer contract in 2017 with a large aerospace company based in Los Angeles. The health system takes on full risk for the care of the company's 5,000 employees who have chosen the MemorialCare accountable care network. "When an employee chooses MemorialCare for the first time, they are required to choose a primary care doctor," Arbuckle notes. "This simple act enables our providers to engage with patients proactively, long before the patient has a need for care."

It is important for patients to understand that they need to stay in-network. Once enrolled with a MemorialCare PCP, patients are issued a sophisticated handheld device from TytoCare called the Home Smart Clinic, which connects the patient's phone with the assigned MemorialCare doctor. The device enables remote physical exams from the home. It can relay a variety of biometrics by functioning as a stethoscope that listens to heart and lung sounds, an otoscope that looks into the ear, a pulse oximeter that measures blood-oxygen levels, and a blood-pressure cuff. A high-definition camera can scan rashes, lesions, and moles to conduct a full dermatological exam. "Young families with children are very engaged with the Home Smart Clinic because of all the health concerns that often happen with kids," Arbuckle says. "It helps them avoid trips to the ER or the doctor's office."

Initiated in 2017, MemorialCare's initial direct-to-employer contractual relationship has proven so successful that it has been extended to 2027. The most recent data show that for the company's covered employee population, MemorialCare has

- reduced inpatient admissions by 30 percent,
- reduced emergency department visits by 47 percent,
- reduced pharmacy expenditures by 22 percent, and
- exceeded patient-satisfaction targets.

MemorialCare has used the success of this relationship to attract 10 additional direct-to-employer contracts. Most recently, the health system has also signed on as the exclusive health system provider for Harmony, United Health Plan's new product focused on accountable care organizations (ACOs), in the South Los Angeles–Orange County region. MemorialCare has rolled out TytoCare's home monitoring device to patients covered by the United Harmony plan.

Other health systems are following the lead of the CMS Innovation Center by investing in infrastructure that positions them for the wholescale implementation of value-based care. Risant Health is a new nonprofit organization created in 2023 by Kaiser Foundation Hospitals to expand and accelerate the adoption of accountable care across the nation. In April 2024, Geisinger Health in Pennsylvania became the first health system to join Risant Health. Geisinger has long been committed to advancing innovation and value-based care models, partnering with other payers, physician groups, and health systems. Geisinger will participate in forming Risant Health's strategy and operational model. Current plans call for Risant Health to acquire four or five more health systems, which will generate an estimated total revenue of $30 billion to $35 billion over the next five years.

Strategies for Health Care Leaders

Many health system executives may feel apprehension about moving entirely to reimbursement under models that no longer focus on volume. At what point should organizations disrupt how they deliver services and position themselves for value-based care?

"Playing in both fields is really tough, because each requires different intentions, infrastructure, and financial incentives," Arbuckle states. "MemorialCare has chosen to go full-bore into accountable care, admittedly at our own financial expense in the early years. We have a budget that we use to keep people healthy, as opposed to the model where we get paid when patients come into the hospital or get sicker. Building this health care infrastructure that touches every access point has put us ahead of most other organizations in terms of meeting CMS's objectives for quality and affordability. It's ultimately a bet on value-based care."

Arbuckle advises that if an organization is truly committed to alternative payment models and willing to incur some financial challenges in the short term, it is better to start the transition sooner rather than later. "Some organizations may have to wait until they have no alternative other than to move over to value-based care," he acknowledges. "In the end, we can't stay in this middle position as a nation much longer."

How should health system leaders prepare to make the transition? "It starts with educating your board of directors and leadership team on what it means to be paid for outcomes and value, rather than volume," Arbuckle says. "It is also critical that your physicians and medical staff leaders not only understand how these payment models work but also buy into them as well."

Two essential components of successful implementation of a value-based model are data collection and analytics. Under a traditional provider perspective, executive leadership looks first at how much of their organization's fee-for-service revenue was used to provide medical care. Greater or higher intensity or volume usually produces a more substantial bottom line. "We look at the medical cost ratio: of the premium dollars we collected, how much did we spend caring for that patient?"

FUTURESCAN SURVEY RESULTS
Disruption

Health care executives from across the nation were asked how likely it is that the following will happen in their hospital or health system by 2030.

By 2030, our hospital or health system will see a 20 percent increase in the number of patients in an accountable care relationship.

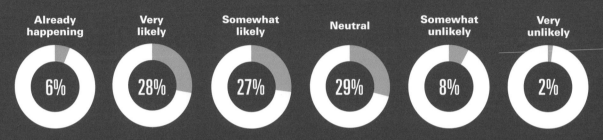

Already happening	Very likely	Somewhat likely	Neutral	Somewhat unlikely	Very unlikely
6%	28%	27%	29%	8%	2%

By 2030, our hospital or health system will enter a strategic partnership to transform or expand our value-based care offering.

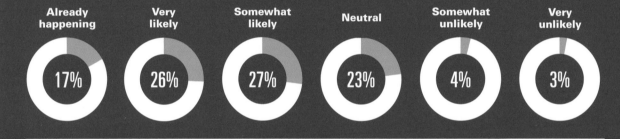

Already happening	Very likely	Somewhat likely	Neutral	Somewhat unlikely	Very unlikely
17%	26%	27%	23%	4%	3%

Arbuckle says. "Our executive leadership team focuses not on volume of services rendered but on prevention, right site of care, and returning the patient to health. The degree to which you can do that cost-effectively affects how you generate a return under value-based care." Arbuckle notes that this analysis requires a great deal of data, including profit and loss by service line and by physician: "It's taken us years to build the data sets that give us the true picture of our medical cost ratio."

When a health system is at full risk for the care of a defined population, it is important to have all the necessary touchpoints along the continuum of care. These include not only medical and behavioral health care services but also post-acute care and home health. Arbuckle advises, "If you don't own it, you can partner on these services through preferential contracts. Be sure your information technology system interfaces with whatever computer systems your partners have."

Arbuckle points out that some care models are not ideal for organizations that are accepting full risk. "Attributed models assign patients to a provider whom they may have seen more than any others. The problem is that patients don't know they have been assigned to a provider in an ACO, and the providers may not know either until the patient needs medical services. When providers don't know they have financial risk for that patient's health, they can't reach out, educate the patient, or do preventive work. And when patients do not intentionally choose an ACO network and provider, they often will not engage." By contrast, in delegated or network models patients intentionally choose the ACO network and their doctor, who can initiate early conversations on preventive health or risk mitigation.

Value-based plans do not have to be HMOs—they can be created around a PPO product. Benefit design is what really matters and has more of an effect on the bottom line of ACOs. For instance, some plans charge patients a $20 copay to visit an urgent care center, but there is no copay to visit the ER. Many patients will opt for the ER because it is less costly to them in the short term. "However, the ER is five times more expensive, and the wait can be five times longer," Arbuckle notes. "This is counterintuitive when trying to find the right site of care." He adds that it is difficult to work with health plans on customizing benefit design because these health plans create products for employers all over the state.

Suggesting ways to cut costs in direct-to-employer contracts can be more easily accomplished and be accretive to the employer and the health system. A team of MemorialCare pharmacists found that some FDA-approved drugs actually are a combination of two over-the-counter medications. A one-month supply of both an over-the-counter pain reliever and a heartburn tablet would cost $35 per month. When those two drugs are combined into one pill that requires a prescription, the cost increases to $1,500 per month. "Our pharmacists have more credibility with our PCPs than even the pharmacy benefit manager, who never flagged this for us or the self-insured employer for whom they worked," Arbuckle says. As a result of MemorialCare's focus on drug spend in this population, the self-insured employer's pharmacy cost trend was a full five percentage points lower than the California statewide average of 10 percent in 2018, 2019, and 2020. Moreover, in the first year of the direct-to-employer relationship, the employer experienced a 21.5 percent decrease in pharmacy spend from the previous year.

It is important to note that the buy-in for value-based care is far from universal. "Some health plans are publicly traded, for-profit companies, and they want to keep premium dollars rather than give them to providers who are willing to take on risk for more shared savings," observes Arbuckle. "Brokers are an important constituency, but they get paid the same amount by health plans whether they just renew the same plan or introduce a new plan that is risky and takes more time. That's when education can play a role."

Over the long term, hospital and health system leaders ultimately expect a transition to value-based care. In the latest *Futurescan* survey, 55 percent of respondents said it is "likely" or "very likely" that their hospital or health system would see a 20 percent increase in the number of patients in an accountable-care relationship over the next five years. Similarly, 53 percent said their organizations would likely enter a strategic partnership by 2030 to transform or expand their value-based care offerings.

Key Takeaways

What are the most important considerations that health care executives should remember when moving their organizations toward value-based care? Arbuckle offers the following suggestions:

- **Be aware that a different infrastructure is required.** "Moving to value-based care is fundamentally a cultural shift," Arbuckle states. "The entire organization needs to adopt a different mindset and accept the shift from a fee-for-service model to a value-based system of care. The data analytics and performance expectations are entirely different in this environment."

- **Understand the criticality of patient engagement and access.** "It is essential to have physical locations and virtual access points throughout your service area," Arbuckle says. "For years, we built our facilities at one address and waited for patients to come to us. That's not the reality anymore."

- **Benefit design matters.** "The ideal is to work with health plans and self-insured employers to incentivize patients to access care in ways that keep them healthy and costs low," Arbuckle says. "An alternative is directly educating patients on lower-cost points of care. That has been a key lesson for us."

Conclusion

As CMS continues to roll out its strategy refresh and its objectives for advancing high-quality, affordable person-centered care, hospitals and health systems nationwide will eventually be called upon to transform how they deliver services. Arbuckle believes that embracing accountable care and building an exclusive network to help keep patients healthy is the right decision for MemorialCare and for consumers in his marketplace. "We think we are well positioned as value-based care continues to accelerate," he declares. "This model may not be right for every health system, but we believe it is ultimately the model of the future."

References

Health Care Payment Learning & Action Network. 2023. "APM Measurement: Progress of Alternative Payment Models—2023 Methodology and Results Report." Published October 26. https://hcp-lan.org/workproducts/apm-methodology-2023.pdf.

The Use of Predictive Technologies to Mitigate Hospital Workforce Shortages

with Roberta L. Schwartz, PhD, MHS, FACHE, executive vice president, Houston Methodist Hospital, and chief innovation officer, Houston Methodist

The rise of artificial intelligence (AI) in the health care setting has been steady and is set to increase rapidly, even as AI continually evolves. There are many reasons for the expanding interest in these technologies, but one eye-popping figure from a McKinsey & Company white paper stands out: the possibility of "$1 trillion of improvement[s]" that health care can capture using them (Bhasker et al. 2023).

The growth in worldwide AI health care technologies will be rapid. These tech companies were valued at $11 billion in 2021 and are expected to reach a $187 billion valuation in 2030 (IBM 2023).

Clearly, AI in health care has arrived, and fully embracing its emergence is Roberta L. Schwartz, PhD, MHS, FACHE, who is the executive vice president of Houston Methodist Hospital and chief innovation officer at Houston Methodist. Consistently named one of the nation's best hospitals, Houston Methodist's hospital system includes an academic medical center, eight community hospitals with a ninth on the way, and more than 2,700 beds throughout the system.

"About six years or so ago, I became really passionate about what I saw was happening in health care innovation and how it could change the way we provide care," Schwartz says. "I became the chief of innovation here and am working to push the technology forward to change the way we do our business." A major element of this innovation is the use of AI, although the term itself is problematic for Schwartz. "It is so genericized at this point, it's nearly a meaningless term," she says.

AI actually comprises a suite of technologies that might be referred to as predictive technologies, large language or deep learning data models, and generative technologies, among other descriptions. Regardless of how they are described, they have emerged as important adjuncts for efficient operation in the hospital setting, and there is likely no more enthusiastic proponent of their use than Schwartz.

Many Potential Uses

Several uses of predictive technologies can affect nonclinical operations (see exhibit 1). But as Schwartz explains, the ongoing shortages of nurses (Haddad

About the Subject Matter Expert

Roberta L. Schwartz, PhD, MHS, FACHE, is the chief innovation officer of the eight-hospital Houston Methodist hospital system, where she works with a team to assess and adopt enterprise-wide emerging digital technologies. Her belief is that health care can be transformed through these new technologies, including various forms of artificial intelligence, patient-focused systems and telemedicine, to create the hospital of the future. Schwartz is also the executive vice president of Houston Methodist Hospital, the system's flagship 979-bed academic hospital, where she oversees all operations.

2023) and advanced practice providers and physicians (Association of American Medical Colleges 2024) are expected to worsen over the next decade just as the number of older patients increases (see exhibit 2).

"The way to look at this problem is the ratio of clinicians to patients," she says. "The ratio is getting worse. We have significant numbers of physicians who are retiring, and we have growing longevity in our patients. You would be stunned at how many people are in this hospital today who are in their 90s and even 100s. It is astounding, and years ago that was not a challenge."

As the number of these patients increases, so does the acuity of their conditions. Years ago, predictions of the future of hospitals suggested that in-hospital care would be similar to a large intensive care unit (ICU). Those predictions were not far off. "Patients that we are treating on the floor today might have been considered ICU patients 10 or 15 years ago," Schwartz says. "We have learned how to take care of more complicated patients in a less acute setting, and we have learned to take care of less acute patients at their homes."

The acuity problem is made worse because the baby boomer population has reached the stage when the need for hospital services is more likely, further stressing hospital clinicians. The cost of health care compounds the problem. "Everyone agrees that health care is too expensive," Schwartz says. "Consumers are demanding lower prices, but with rising labor and supply costs, there is no way to do all of this work at a lesser price. Even if we did things the exact same way, with inflation, it just keeps going up."

She adds, "The only path forward is innovation."

Help for Stressed Clinicians

Reducing the workload on overburdened clinicians is key to mitigating workforce shortages. One way to free up clinician time is by using predictive technologies to create personalized risk profiles for patients that more accurately determine when follow-up is needed.

"Predictive technologies now allow you to not only look at a risk profile but also compare it to other Medicare patient records in order to develop a personalized profile," Schwartz says. "This allows us to identify who needs to see the patient, when, and for what issues, and it allows us to pick out, say, the eight patients of 1,000 that we need to be especially concerned about." Schwartz points out that personalized risk profiles put the clinical focus on the patients who truly need the attention, freeing up clinical time elsewhere.

Another time-saver is the use of remote monitoring sensors or buttons. Remote monitoring keeps patients essentially tethered to the hospital, which monitors relevant data as they come in. Remote monitoring has been used for a while now, but it has focused on specific disease states. For example, a heart failure patient would be remotely monitored for specific cardiovascular signs. This fragmented, disease-specific approach will change, Schwartz predicts, into a single, common platform over the next five years, thereby widening the range of data that can be easily monitored remotely.

Reducing the Documentation Load

Clinicians routinely bemoan the amount of time needed to complete clinical notes. In surveying its nurses, Houston Methodist found that as much as half their time was spent on documentation. In response, Houston Methodist aggressively attacked the problem by installing a large telenursing program designed to support its nurses on the floor. Schwartz explains: "We asked the nurses, 'If we could take away one burden, what would it be?' And we figured out that they needed the most help with admission and discharge paperwork."

Schwartz and her colleagues initiated a pilot study (Schwartz et al. 2024) to explore the feasibility of a large-scale telenursing program in which admissions and discharge paperwork are completed virtually. Investigations determined that interruptions on the nursing floor commonly stretched the time needed to complete admissions and discharge paperwork to 45 minutes, whereas a centralized telenurse system

---

Exhibit 1

Potential Nonclinical Uses of Predictive Technologies in Hospital Settings

Generate standardized communications to both providers and patients
Create performance reports
Respond to requests for proposals
Review shifting legal risks and regulations
Help marketing and sales staff analyze customer data and build sales campaigns
Better inform chatbots that tend to nonclinical queries

Exhibit 2

Projected Physician Shortages by 2034

Clinician type	Range of shortage
Primary care physicians	−17,800 to −48,000
Specialty physicians	−21,000 to −77,100
Surgical specialists	−15,800 to −30,200
Medical specialists	−3,800 to −13,400
Other specialists	−10,300 to −35,600

Source: Association of American Medical Colleges (2021).

could complete it in 13 minutes. This time saving allowed the telenursing staff to carefully review the documentation, sometimes making "great catches, from listing incorrect pharmacies to noting possible drug interactions," Schwartz says. "The new set of eyes is important, and the nurse on the floor now has time to address the fact that the patient down the hall has not had lunch or the one next door hasn't had their phlebotomy yet."

Paperwork is also completed much more thoroughly with this system. Schwartz tells a story of the Spiritual Care department wondering why the requests from patients for visits had spiked by as much as two-thirds. The reason: Virtual admissions nurses filled out the section on spiritual care, whereas the nurses on the floor didn't have time and often skipped the nonclinical question.

In-Room Cameras and Centralized Monitoring

Schwartz is passionate about an innovation that is rolling out at Houston Methodist: fixed digital cameras. Picture this scenario: A nurse requires a second nurse to sign off on his or her review of a patient's high-risk medications and blood products. Often, the nurse will stand in the patient's doorway, gloves on, and ask fellow staff, "Can I get a nurse to help with this patient?" These important reviews require signoff by two nurses as a safety measure, but a second nurse is not always immediately available, so the nurse requiring signoff will stay at the door looking for their partner nurses. An internal review by Houston Methodist found that locating a second nurse can sometimes take 5 to 15 minutes—more time wasted. This situation, according to Schwartz, is painful for nurses.

This situation has been ameliorated by Epic's electronic health record, which now allows a virtual nurse to complete the signoff. But, instead of the nurse in the room being armed with an iPad through which the virtual nurse might work, a much more maneuverable end-point camera, which is set up in

the room and connected to a high-definition television, will monitor care and allow the nurse to respond from a centralized location.

"The ability to control health care machines from afar is coming to a system near you," Schwartz advises. "I believe that in five to 10 years every room and every patient room will have end-point cameras. A new level of oversight of every patient will be possible through this technology." Virtual clinical rounding is another planned advancement.

A Boon for Rural and Urban Hospitals

For a large, big-city medical center, the expense of implementing this type of camera-based, centralized monitoring program might be borne by patient loads, but what about a small rural hospital? How do those hospitals save nursing time with a system like this? According to Schwartz, this type of system might be even more critical for smaller hospitals with low bed counts.

"We recently hosted the governor's delegation with some key state senators from Texas," she says. "One woman from a rural area said that this type of technology could have saved her. She had to close down services due to a lack of nursing. Rural areas need this type of support, and it's even more essential for these hospitals to jump in." The utility

of these systems is already established, she adds, since they are currently used in some prisons. "We have virtual centers set up to support the prisons, and we are going to need these systems for certain hospitals in rural areas."

What about remote monitoring for urban hospitals? "Our centralized support covers all eight of our hospitals over various geographies," Schwartz explains. "We don't lack patients, but we need to know when patients don't need to be transferred. It could be that what is needed for that patient has been done at the current location, or the expense is not justified, or we need to transfer that patient very quickly. We are making these kinds of decisions regarding strokes in all of our hospitals and in the ICU."

To support that level of remote monitoring requires a robust monitoring center, which at Houston Methodist looks akin to an air traffic control center.

Lives—and Money—Saved

As the hospital system gains remote-monitoring experience and data, Schwartz has been able to point to undeniable successes. For example, ICU code blues decreased by 20 percent following the advent of virtual ICU monitoring. That means both money and lives have been saved.

In addition, discharge nurses have been removed because the centralized staff now performs that function—another significant savings. Locum tenens nursing—a major financial burden—has been eliminated. Houston Methodist also employed mobility techs, who walk patients on a scheduled basis because the nursing staff does not have the time. Those roles are now being reduced in the system.

Nurses appreciate the new system. "I asked a nurse how the program was going, and she said, 'Amazing,' and told me a story," Schwartz explains. "The nurse said she was working with a patient who seemed fine, but then a nurse practitioner [NP] came in the room and told her that her patient was in trouble. The nurse said no, he's fine, but the NP insisted that he was not. They did some lab work and found that the patient was indeed in trouble—something the trending from wearable monitoring technology had discovered. In some cases, these monitoring technologies are picking up concerning data 12 to 18 hours in advance of nurses on the floor."

The use of AI in-room end-point cameras and predictive technologies has increased the accuracy of room scheduling, with the number of cases in some sites now have increased cases in the same room hours by over 15 percent.

A Boon for Patients

Schwartz lists five ways in which these predictive technologies can help patients:

1. **Convenience**—Get patients home or where they need to go more quickly, and monitor them at home instead of in the hospital.
2. **Identification**—Detecting deterioration in a patient's status earlier saves lives.
3. **Providing health care**—As in the example of rural hospitals that need to shut down because they do not have the health care personnel to run a specific service, remote monitoring can be used to provide health care when otherwise there would be none.
4. **Overcoming transportation issues**—It can be very complicated

for certain patients to get to a health care site in both rural and urban environments, making remote monitoring essential. The more difficult a patient's transportation situation is, the less likely they are to seek care. No-show rates for follow-up clinics can range from 30 to 50 percent, Schwartz notes.

5. **Better health care**—Remote monitoring often leads to care that is better than traditional care. "Often, I think these technologies are motivating people to do the right thing," Schwartz says.

Return on Investment

Houston Methodist's Center for Innovation always aims for a three-to-one return on investment (ROI). "That's our goal," Schwartz says. "Unless you are going to substantially change the quality of health care, we are not going to do anything that doesn't have at least a one-to-one ROI. From there, we would try to drive up the ROI closer to three to one."

The challenge with innovation is not so much the technology as its implementation. Innovation will change models of care, which allows for the stretching of bedside ratios without sacrificing quality and improves the quality of work-life for staff such as nurses and physicians.

"Change is hard. Someone said the definition of a transformation is a butterfly that comes from a caterpillar—what develops is unrecognizable from how it started," Schwartz says. "As I was told, never underestimate the ability of the body's immune system to fight off change. People dislike change."

How, then, to motivate staff? "You always have to go back to the 'why,'" Schwartz explains. "Why are we doing this? What will it give us? As a leader, you have to remind yourself that people need to be consistently reminded of the why." One ROI metric is the ability to treat more patients by reducing wasted time.

Key Takeaways

Schwartz offers the following takeaways for leaders considering the adoption of new technology:

• Technologies employing various elements of AI are already serving hospitals, and more are coming soon. Several systems are mature products, and others are still evolving. In addition to many nonclinical applications, there are several AI-enhanced technologies that will greatly mitigate the workforce shortages that already exist and are increasing. Leaders need to dedicate personnel to implement and study AI-enhanced technologies.

FUTURESCAN SURVEY RESULTS
Predictive Technologies

Health care executives from across the nation were asked how likely it is that the following will happen in their hospital or health system by 2030.

By 2030, discussions between patients and caregivers will be automatically summarized using voice technology.

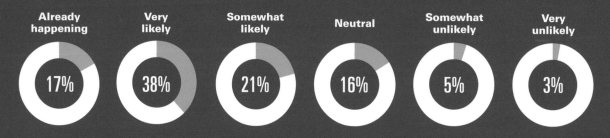

Already happening	Very likely	Somewhat likely	Neutral	Somewhat unlikely	Very unlikely
17%	38%	21%	16%	5%	3%

By 2030, our Department of Health and Human Services caregivers will use advanced and specific biosensor information to augment their clinical decisions for both inpatient and outpatient individuals (e.g., vital signs, temperature, pulse oxygen monitoring).

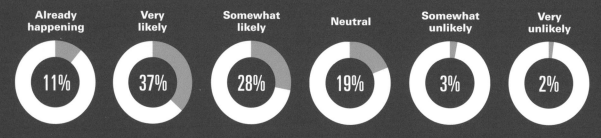

Already happening	Very likely	Somewhat likely	Neutral	Somewhat unlikely	Very unlikely
11%	37%	28%	19%	3%	2%

- The use of predictive technologies in clinical settings helps both patients (improved evidence-based health care) and clinicians (reduced stress from tedious tasks). Both groups should be made aware of the benefits of these technologies.
- Change management is the most difficult aspect of transforming your workforce, and it is never too early to begin that work, even if you are still evaluating different technological solutions.

References

Association of American Medical Colleges. 2024. "The Complexities of Physician Supply and Demand: Projections From 2021 to 2036." GlobalData Plc. Published March. http://aamc.org/media/75236/download?attachment.

Bhasker, S., D. Bruce, J. Lamb, and G. Stein. 2023. "Tackling Healthcare's Biggest Burdens With Generative AI." McKinsey & Co. Published July 10. http://mckinsey.com/industries/healthcare/our-insights/tackling-healthcares-biggest-burdens-with-generative-ai.

Haddad, L. M., P. Annamaraju, and T. J. Toney-Butler. 2023. "Nursing Shortage." StatPearls. Published February 13. https://www.ncbi.nlm.nih.gov/books/NBK493175.

IBM Education. 2023. "AI Healthcare Benefits." Published July 11. https://www.ibm.com/blog/the-benefits-of-ai-in-healthcare.

Schwartz, R. L., S. K. Hamlin, G. M. Vozzella, L. N. Randle, S. Klahn, G. J. Maris, and A. D. Waterman. 2024. "Utilizing Telenursing to Supplement Acute Care Nursing in an Era of Workforce Shortages." *CIN: Computers, Informatics, Nursing* 42(2): 151–57.

Local Voices Can Strengthen Impact of Community Programs

with Len M. Nichols, PhD, nonresident fellow, Urban Institute; professor emeritus of health policy, George Mason University

Hospitals and health systems have a long-standing commitment to serve the health needs of their communities. Over the past decade, that commitment and the underlying activities have expanded to include leading and supporting programs and services that are designed to improve health—both directly and indirectly—for patients and communities. There has also been increasing awareness and understanding that social factors have a significant effect on individuals' ability to achieve good health.

"After the Affordable Care Act was passed, it became clear very quickly that readmission penalties are not caused by what went on in the hospital but by what didn't happen outside of the hospital," says Len Nichols, PhD, professor emeritus of health policy at George Mason University. "That had the effect of focusing hospitals' attention upstream in a way it had not been before." The awareness that social determinants of health (SDOH) and racial disparities negatively affect health has led many hospitals and health systems to create

initiatives aimed at addressing these realities.

The Current Health Care Landscape

Hospitals and health systems have embraced the mission of addressing SDOH and racial health inequities on a large scale and are collaborating with community partners to do so. Some have even adopted an "anchor mission": using their economic power as large employers in their communities to create jobs and wealth among businesses

owned by disadvantaged populations. These initiatives address the low wages, lack of fresh food, homelessness, and other SDOHs to raise the standard of living and enhance access to health care. By taking the data and insights gathered through the community health needs assessment (CHNA) process, hospitals and health systems can make strong commitments to address and improve social determinants. This work is foundational to increasing access and improving overall health and wellness. "If you don't have economic viability

About the Subject Matter Expert

Len M. Nichols, PhD, is a nonresident fellow in the Health Policy Center of the Urban Institute and a professor emeritus of health policy at George Mason University. Len has been intimately involved in health reform debates, policy development, and communication with the media and policymakers for 30 years, after he was senior advisor for health policy at the Office of Management and Budget in the first two years of the Clinton administration. Through testimony, publications, public speaking, and

technical advice, he has helped shape the opinions of policymakers, researchers, journalists, and policy analysts. Len's current research focus is on incentivizing collaborative financing of social determinants of health. Len has served on the board of directors of the National Committee for Quality Assurance and has been an advisor to various state and federal policy agencies. He received his PhD in economics from the University of Illinois in 1980.

or basic resources, everything else is a Band-Aid," Nichols asserts. "Anchor institutions are thinking outside the box and addressing problems upstream." The Healthcare Anchor Network is a national collaboration among more than 70 leading health care systems with over 1,000 hospitals that are building more inclusive and sustainable local economies.

Nichols says that engaging with local residents to learn what their priorities are has been one of the biggest community benefit trends over the last 20 years. "A much more collaborative process has emerged, which includes engaging community stakeholders in the design of the interventions and the evaluation—that is, what we measure to define success. This has led to much better relationships and outcomes," he observes.

Many health systems have focused on food, housing, and transportation. "They may want to consider strategies for how they can impact the full panoply of social determinants, which includes economic viability," notes Nichols. One example of an initiative that is aimed at building local wealth is Evergreen Cooperative Laundry (ECL). In 2018, Cleveland Clinic and ECL entered into an agreement for the cooperative to take over management of the health system's laundry facility in Cleveland's low-income Collinwood neighborhood. The expansion brought more than 100 new hires into the employee-owned ECL, joining the 50 workers who were already employed at its original laundry facility. ECL now handles more than 19 million pounds of laundry for the health system each year, which has strengthened the local economy.

"This is a model that can work for other hospitals," Nichols declares. "Think about whom you can train locally for all kinds of jobs in the health care ecosystem. Nursing assistants, aides, dietary workers—all these jobs are within the purview of health care hiring practices. They should become part of operations."

For example, in 2021 New Orleans–based Ochsner Health entered into an agreement with contractor Trax

Development to create SafeSource Direct. The resulting enterprise manufactures, warehouses, and distributes personal protective equipment (PPE) for health care. The $150 million investment developed two facilities: one that houses its headquarters in Lafayette Parish, and a new 400,000-square-foot manufacturing facility in St. Martin Parish. The collaboration overall created 2,200 new jobs in Louisiana's Acadiana region and meets a national demand for a reliable domestic source of PPE. It also builds on Ochsner Health's commitment of $465 million to improve the health and lives of people in the Acadiana community.

CommonSpirit Health: A Case Study

CommonSpirit is a large health system doing innovative work in addressing the social, economic, and environmental determinants of health by leveraging the strength and capacity of the health system in partnership with community-based organizations (CBOs). Based in Chicago, CommonSpirit operates in 24 states and has created a comprehensive model called the Connected Community Network (CCN). The model is based on two realities: First, when patients receive the social resources they need, they are less likely to be readmitted to the hospital, and their overall health can be improved. Second, by

better tracking the social interventions and care that patients need after returning to their homes, services and support can be targeted to ensure that patients' total health and well-being improve and that gaps in care can be better mitigated.

Three key principles form the foundation of the CCN model:

1. The co-creation of shared vision and solutions in collaboration with all key community stakeholders.
2. The establishment of community governance that relies on local decision-making. Solutions are place based and support cross-sector collaborations and partnerships.
3. The galvanizing of community support and pooled resources via a community bank. This model allows multiple diverse organizations across sectors to blend private and public funding to accomplish the shared vision and solutions.

CCNs connect a network of providers and CBOs through a referral system and technology platform that increases points of access, tracks outcomes, and manages reimbursement. CCNs also advance health equity by bringing community stakeholders and resources to underserved populations in need of vital services. At the heart of the local CCN is the most unique component of the model: a neutral community convener

who functions as the facilitator, brings together local provider organizations, establishes a governance structure, and manages network funding. The convener advocates for the CCN and aligns it with local needs and initiatives. Since its introduction in 2016, the model has expanded to include more community-based partners and broader stakeholders, which has positioned CommonSpirit to pursue other community-centered models as well.

CommonSpirit has partnered with Pathways Community HUB Institute (PCHI), a national nonprofit that has developed an effective model to help communities work together to support their underserved populations. In 2021 CommonSpirit and PCHI implemented a community-centric care navigation model in six communities in Nevada, Arizona, California, Texas, and Nebraska. In four of the five states, community stakeholders identified Black maternal and fetal health as two of their top health priorities, as well as metrics that can be tracked quickly to aid understanding of the model's benefits.

Over the last three years, Common Spirit has invested $1.9 million in PCHI communities, an investment that motivated other organizations and entities to contribute an additional $12.1 million. This makes a total investment of over $14 million in SDOH infrastructure to address health equity initiatives in these communities—money that otherwise would not have been generated. This is important because, while hospitals can play an important role in addressing SDOH issues, a variety of community partners and government entities also need to be involved to strengthen the social safety net.

"What distinguishes this effort is the fact that CommonSpirit really believes in bringing local community voices to the table and listening to them," Nichols says. "CommonSpirit has embraced the input from key stakeholders and believe their SDOH initiatives will work better because those who are affected are part of the planning and design process. They know what the real barriers to better outcomes are."

Expanding the concept of community benefit is clearly on the minds of health care leaders across the country. In the latest *Futurescan* survey conducted in spring 2024, a sizeable number of respondents envision broadening the types of activities in which their organizations invest to enhance the health of their communities. Thirty-seven percent of surveyed leaders said it was "very or somewhat likely" that their hospital or health system would "create a nontraditional community benefit, such as developing a business venture or providing financial heft to community or economic development efforts." Another 22 percent said that this was "already happening" in their organization. On another query, nearly half of respondents—47 percent—said it was "very or somewhat likely" that their hospital or health system's community benefit would be defined not only by charitable care but also by economic impact (e.g., new job creation, community development projects outside of health care). Twenty-six percent said this was already the case in their institutions.

Strategies for Health Care Leaders

As suggested by the *Futurescan* survey, many hospitals and health systems are already considering investments in activities that address SDOH and vital community health initiatives. Nichols believes the intended purpose of community benefit activity should be to promote the health and well-being of every individual and community in the United States. He says, "There needs to be a societal acknowledgement that housing, food insecurity, and social and economic needs impact both physical and mental health. The health care system catches what comes downstream. Why not devote resources upstream to reduce widely known drivers of poor health and work to keep individuals out of the hospital?"

Momentum is growing for a national discussion not only about what should constitute community benefits and how health care dollars should be spent but also about how community partners can best collaborate to impact individuals' ability to achieve better health. The National Academy of Medicine has released a report that emphasizes the need for a bold vision and sustainable financing strategies to prioritize health and well-being for all (National Academy of Medicine 2024).

The Partnership to Align Social Care was established to advance the Centers for Medicare and Medicaid Services Innovation Center's strategy refresh, which supports the transformation of health- and community-centered social care delivery systems and enables value-based care. This new strategy explores a redesign of roles in the evolving health and social ecosystem, including the roles that hospitals, health plans, the government, and CBOs should play

Health care executives from across the nation were asked how likely it is that the following will happen in their hospital or health system by 2030.

By 2030, our hospital or health system will create a nontraditional community benefit, such as developing a business venture or providing financial heft to community/economic development efforts.

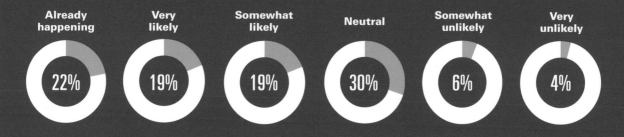

Already happening	Very likely	Somewhat likely	Neutral	Somewhat unlikely	Very unlikely
22%	19%	19%	30%	6%	4%

By 2030, our hospital or health system's community benefit will be defined not only by charitable care, but also by economic impact (e.g., new job creation, non–health care community development projects).

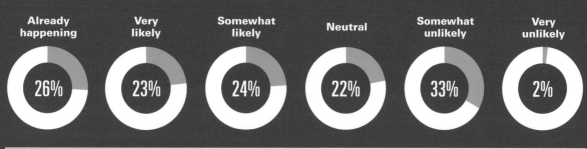

Already happening	Very likely	Somewhat likely	Neutral	Somewhat unlikely	Very unlikely
26%	23%	24%	22%	33%	2%

in promoting well-being. It is funded by health systems and health plans and includes representation from those sectors, the Administration for Community Living, and other agencies within the US Department of Health and Human Services.

A bipartisan, bicameral group of legislators at the federal level, known as the Congressional Social Determinants of Health Caucus, has also been convened to explore opportunities to improve the impact of services that address SDOH with the support of federal funding. The Caucus is collecting input from CBOs, health care providers, public health and social service organizations, and state and local government leaders on how best to facilitate effective SDOH interventions and how Congress can take action to advance this work.

Nichols emphasizes that grassroots efforts in the local community can have a big impact overall. "Genuine social equity requires efforts to make communities economically viable and sustainable, and that will require attention to investment, purchasing, job and career training, and employment recruitment efforts," he notes. "Can you train local moms or formerly incarcerated individuals to become community health workers with a career path that aspires to more specialized health care support roles? Can you buy goods and services from locally owned laundry and supply companies to keep health care dollars circulating in the community? These are ways to benefit the local population that fall directly in line with the operation of a hospital."

Key Considerations

For health care executives who are considering how to make an impact, Nichols suggests the following strategies as a starting point.

- Do not be intimidated by the scale of needs within a community. "It is important to start somewhere and start now," Nichols notes. "Prioritize the greatest need and look to peers for successful programs, models, and best practices. You don't need to reinvent the wheel. Hospitals and health systems are increasingly stepping up to help address public health challenges that would otherwise be left unmet. If in doubt, start with medically tailored meals for frequent emergency department users. You cannot go wrong by providing nutritious fare for patients who may live in food deserts or are surrounded by fast food establishments."
- Listen to your local community. Hospitals and health systems already engage community partners through the CHNA process.

"Many organizations are moving beyond discussion by partnering with community stakeholders to contribute to the design of programs and services. They are proactively seeking a better understanding of the role that the hospital or health system can play in improving access to the social determinants that lead to better health," Nichols says. "Not only does this engage the right people in your initiatives and invest them in the outcomes; it will also help you see which services are most important to truly benefit the community you serve."

- Consider involving a community-health or social worker in the leadership of programs designed to meet SDOH. Nichols speaks from his own personal experiences. "Social and community-health workers see and understand needs differently than doctors, nurses, or other health care professionals," he states. "You want to involve those who are closest to the patients and community members you are trying to help and who are closest to the challenge you are trying to meet. Involve individuals who understand the world as it is and also how it can be better. I have never failed to learn a great deal from every community health or social worker I have met in my last eight years of doing work on addressing SDOH."

Conclusion

"The magnitude of patient and community health needs isn't diminishing," Nichols observes. "Fortunately, there is a greater understanding of the factors that can impede one's ability to achieve better health. Health care organizations are making a substantial impact on the overall health of their communities by addressing SDOH. These initiatives go far beyond charity care or traditional community benefit activities. By working to address identified health challenges and the unmet needs in your local market, hospitals and health systems can become powerful catalysts for change that uplifts entire populations and invests in the health and well-being of all members of your community."

References

National Academy of Medicine. 2024. *Valuing America's Health: Aligning Financing to Reward Better Health and Well-Being.* Washington, DC: The National Academies Press. https://doi.org/10.17226/27141.

Healthcare Employees' Changing Expectations

with Hanna Patterson, Senior Vice President of Health Care and Applied Learning, Guild

Workforce challenges continue to be one of the foremost concerns of health care leaders across the country. In addition to staffing shortages at all levels, the United States is seeing the most diverse working population ever: four different generations with varying priorities now compose the US workforce (Kumar 2023). While baby boomers seek job security, Gen Xers look for work-life balance and upward mobility in their careers. Millennials and Gen Zers want to align with their employers' ethics while also maintaining work–life balance.

With all of the diverse expectations of these generational cohorts, how can C-suite leaders attract prospective employees and retain current ones? Hanna Patterson, senior vice president of healthcare and applied learning teams at Guild, suggests first and foremost that health care leaders listen to prospective and current employees about what is most important to them.

The Current Health Care Landscape

"One of the most notable changes we are seeing is that employees are looking for more flexibility," Patterson says. "This may include more time off or flexible scheduling, such as shorter or longer work shifts." Family demands or school

schedules are often driving this need. Patterson says that staff members also want their employers to take a real interest in their growth and development. "Even if people already have the skills for their current job, things are changing rapidly, such as the increasing applications of artificial intelligence. Health care employees know that with innovative technology, treatments, and care models, they need to learn new skills over the course of their careers." A 2024 Guild survey of its health care clients highlights this trend: 86 percent of its client organizations' workers felt they needed more education to achieve their career goals.

Millennials and Gen Zers are also looking for more purpose. They want to believe that there is more meaning to the time they spend working than simply making money. Gen Zers especially want greater work–life balance. Patterson notes that the vast majority of workers, regardless of their generation, would prefer to stay with their current employer if their needs are being met.

Strategies for Health Care Leaders

"With all these varying dynamics, organizations need to be more nimble and evolve more quickly in order to attract

About the Subject Matter Expert

Hanna Patterson is the senior vice president of health care and applied learning at Guild. In her role, Patterson works with over 25 organizations in leading a mission to innovate talent development through diverse educational approaches. Prior to joining Guild, Hanna worked at Deloitte Consulting, where she spearheaded the firm's market position on the future of health and worked at the intersection of health care and social impact. She has been a featured speaker at Women Deliver and is a published author in *Modern Healthcare*. She holds a bachelor's degree from Northwestern University and a master of business administration degree from the University of Texas McCombs School of Business.

and retain top talent," Patterson states. "For instance, one organization decided to focus on how it could use virtual care to retain older, more experienced nurses. Because of the often intense physical demands of nursing, this model allows nurses to participate in a care team remotely, reducing the physical work load while enabling registered nurses (RNs) to perform at the top of their licenses."

One of the most notable trends is the shift in how health care organizations are choosing to invest in employees' careers. Hospitals and health systems have traditionally offered tuition reimbursement to employees who want to advance their careers. However, this system requires students to pay for tuition up front, and many entry-level employees cannot afford to do so. As a result, the employees who could advance educationally under this system were primarily nurses and administrators. "If you want entry-level or lower-paid workers to benefit from education, consider making payments directly to the school on their behalf," advises Patterson. "These workers are essentially your next generation of talent, and you want them to advance their knowledge and skills because they can fulfill future needs, such as for nurses and pharmacists."

As an example, Bon Secours Mercy Health (BSMH) in Cincinnati has created its own talent pipeline for entry-level workers and has successfully graduated them to higher-level positions. BSMH's program includes tuition-free programs, clinical career pathways, and personalized coaching. A dedicated internal mobility team at BSMH supports the effort in two ways: by matching appropriate roles to employees who are seeking career growth and by collaborating with internal leaders across the organization to identify and fill talent gaps. The most popular career tracks have been those that lead to careers as medical assistants, phlebotomy technicians, and nurses. A similarly popular track helps current nurses obtain a bachelor's degree. Nearly a third of enrollees have been promoted since the program's inception in 2022. The efforts

of BSMH's internal mobility team have been instrumental in creating a culture of growth and opportunity at the health system, ensuring that the investment in education translates into tangible career pathways for employees.

Some health care organizations are increasing their capacity for on-site, real-time experiences to further prepare current employees for placement and ensure that they meet the qualifications for licensure. Nursing departments have had clinical rotations for years, but other professionals also need hands-on training, such as phlebotomists who require training for drawing blood. Midlevel employees, such as medical assistants and nursing aides, can benefit from job-shadowing opportunities. "Didactic classwork is only part of the equation," says Patterson. "Think about how your organization can provide learning opportunities beyond the classroom."

Promoting the benefits of education and an organization's commitment to it is becoming an effective recruitment strategy. "Painting a picture of opportunity and advancement supported by employer-paid training sends a very different message than 'We are hiring you for this one job,'" Patterson states. "Talent acquisition teams have greater success in filling hard-to-find positions when they share career pathways with applicants that go beyond their current career aspirations and lock them in for the long haul."

Equity, Inclusion, and Community Benefit

Because of staffing shortages, some health care organizations are reconsidering populations they might have previously discounted. Patterson posits, "Do all new employees need to have a high school diploma? Can you hire personnel in their late teens or early 20s for transport or janitorial positions and pay for them to acquire their high school equivalency certificate? Alternatively, can you bring on skilled immigrants from the Middle East or South America and provide English classes to help them integrate into their jobs?"

In terms of keeping an open dialogue, Patterson suggests that C-suite executives be proactive: "Some employees want to understand the values of the organization, so leaders should be communicative about them. Others want to be listened to and heard." This is especially important if a hospital or health system is facing a movement to unionize.

Another expectation that is increasingly important in the workplace is equity and inclusion. A recent study revealed that 80 percent of the American RN population was white (Smiley et al. 2023). Patterson adds that these are often older women and that the workforce demographics of some hospitals and health systems do not match their communities at large. "In

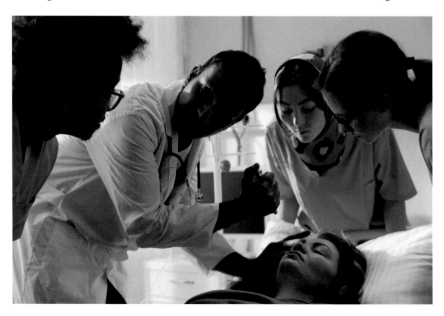

FUTURESCAN SURVEY RESULTS
Workforce

Health care executives from across the nation were asked how likely it is that the following will happen in their hospital or health system by 2030.

By 2030, our hospital or health system will have increased its financial investment in solutions to attract and retain employees by 50 percent.

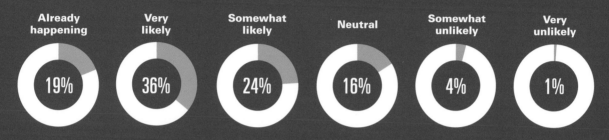

Already happening	Very likely	Somewhat likely	Neutral	Somewhat unlikely	Very unlikely
19%	36%	24%	16%	4%	1%

By 2030, 100 percent of employees will report they strongly agree or agree that our organization supports their career goals.

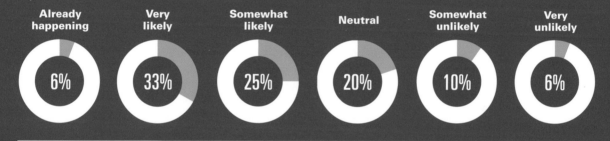

Already happening	Very likely	Somewhat likely	Neutral	Somewhat unlikely	Very unlikely
6%	33%	25%	20%	10%	6%

many organizations, there is diversity in lower-level roles but not in management positions," she declares. "Hospital leaders may want to explore ways to offer these employees the opportunity to advance into higher-level roles." Providing a pathway for employees to achieve better economic outcomes for themselves and their families also has a significant positive effect on an organization's community.

One health system concluded that there was a need to further develop a more equitable and representative talent pipeline within its nursing population to better serve the diverse needs of its patients and community. As one solution to addressing this need, the health system included a fully funded prelicensure nursing program in its educational offerings. The initiative reduced barriers to entry and created accessible pathways for Black and Hispanic employees, encouraging greater enrollment from these underrepresented groups. By removing financial and logistical obstacles, the program sought to attract a more diverse pool of nursing candidates, aligning the demographics of the nursing workforce more closely with those of the patient population and the broader employee base. In two years, there was

fourfold increase in the representation of Black and Hispanic students enrolled in the program compared to the existing nursing population.

"These initiatives have significant community benefit implications for entire populations," states Patterson. "Education, income, and job opportunities are all major factors in health access and quality of life. Health systems are often an area's largest employer and can make significant improvements in these social determinants of health. Some hospitals are actually including these initiatives in their community benefits reporting. By striving to move underrepresented populations into more patient-facing roles, hospitals are also seeing better outcomes, since there is more trust when care teams look like their patients."

Key Takeaways

The commitment of health care leaders to address their staffing challenges was underscored by the results of the 2024 *Futurescan* survey, in which 60 percent of respondents said it was "very likely" or "somewhat likely" that by 2030 their organizations will have increased their financial investment in attracting and retaining employees by 50 percent. Fifty-seven percent believed that it was "very likely" or "somewhat likely" that by 2030 all their employees would report that their organization supported employees' career goals. Six percent of respondents said this was already the case.

As health care leaders invest in ways to successfully recruit and retain a dynamic workforce, Patterson suggests they keep the following principles in mind:

- **A majority of employees want to stay with their employers.** "If health care organizations invest in helping employees advance their careers, they stand a better chance of stabilizing and growing their workforce," Patterson says.
- **Have a vision for where your workforce is headed.** "Although many organizations are focused on current worker shortages, it is also important to define the types of

positions and care team models your organization will need for the future," Patterson says. "By clearly defining its long-term needs, organizations can encourage people to pursue jobs that will be needed in the future. There is a lot of power in taking ownership and creating a workforce that best matches your long-term vision."

- **Think differently about where to find your future employees.** "Organizations can no longer recruit their way out of staffing shortages," says Patterson. "The status quo is inefficient and ineffective. There will always be the opportunity to recruit new graduates, but other pipelines of talent are needed. Entry-level employees can be nurtured. High-level talent that may be overpriced by health care standards—such as cybersecurity—can also be grown by finding the right existing employees."

Conclusion

Patterson states that the commonality among health care organizations that are doing well in managing their workforce is that they have leaders who see the need to meet changing employee expectations by using nontraditional strategies. "They are looking at recruitment and retention differently and realize the need to get out of the arms race," she says, referring to strategies that are heavy on pay raises, sign-on bonuses, and other financial incentives. "By meeting the moment and really listening, health care leaders can help employees feel that they are being treated fairly and that their concerns have been heard. Of course, it's ultimately critical that hospitals and health systems meet employee demands for flexibility, career advancement, meaningful work, and a healthy work–life balance."

References

Kumar, V. S. 2023. "Gen Z in the Workplace: How Should Companies Adapt?" Johns Hopkins University. Published April 18. https://imagine.jhu.edu/blog/2023/04/18/gen-z-in-the-workplace-how-should-companies-adapt.

Smiley, R., R. Allgeyer, Y. Shobo, K. C. Lyons, R. Letourneau, E. Zhong, N. Kaminski-Ozturk, and M. Alexander. 2023. "The 2022 National Nursing Workforce Survey." *Journal of Nursing Regulation* 14(1): S1–S90. https://www.journalofnursingregulation.com/article/S2155-8256(23)00047-9/fulltext.

ABOUT THE CONTRIBUTORS

Society for Health Care Strategy & Market Development

The Society for Health Care Strategy & Market Development (SHSMD), a professional membership group of the AHA, is the largest and most prominent voice for health care strategists. SHSMD serves strategists across diverse disciplines, providing essential knowledge, leading-edge tools and invaluable connections. SHSMD empowers members to overcome obstacles, foresee the future and drive change, towards the vision of a world with healthier people and communities achieved through bold, actionable and inclusive strategies. For more information about *Futurescan*, contact SHSMD at 312.422.3888 or shsmd@aha.org.

American College of Healthcare Executives/Health Administration Press

The American College of Healthcare Executives is an international professional society of more than 49,000 healthcare executives who lead hospitals, healthcare systems and other healthcare organizations. ACHE's mission is to advance its members and healthcare management excellence. ACHE offers its prestigious FACHE® credential, signifying board certification in healthcare management. ACHE's established network of 76 chapters provides access to networking, education and career development at the local level. In addition, ACHE is known for its magazine, *Healthcare Executive*, and its career development and public policy programs. Through such efforts, ACHE works toward its vision of being the preeminent professional society for leaders dedicated to improving health.

The Foundation of the American College of Healthcare Executives was established to further advance healthcare management excellence through education and research. The Foundation of ACHE is known for its educational programs—including the annual Congress on Healthcare Leadership, which draws more than 4,000 participants—and groundbreaking research. Its publishing division, Health Administration Press, is one of the largest publishers of books and journals on health services management, including textbooks for college and university courses. For more information, visit www.ache.org.